The Lazy Man's Way To Enlightenment

What You're Looking For Is What Is Looking

David A. Bhodan

Right Now
Publishing

Right Now Publishing

ISBN-13: 978-0615838106
ISBN-10: 0615838103

First Printing, 2012
Printed in the United States of America

Contents

Dedication   v

Preface   ix

Introduction   xiv

Chapter 1 – A Case of Mistaken Identity   1

Chapter 2 – Lost in Translation   11

Chapter 3 – The Price of Admission   16

Chapter 4 – Enlightenment Isn't What You Think   23

Chapter 5 – Belief Drops Away   30

Chapter 6 – Look Until It Is Seen   37

Chapter 7 – What Is Real   45

Chapter 8 – The Granddaddy Illusion   51

Chapter 9 – A Timeless Now   57

Chapter 10 – Fear, Guilt & Shame   61

Chapter 11 – Everything Is Appearance Only   69

Chapter 12 – Present Before Thought   75

Chapter 13 – Oh, What Webs We Weave   80

Chapter 14 – The Essence of What Is   84

Chapter 15 – Thinking   89

Chapter 16 – One Without A Second   95

Chapter 17 – The Elusive Obvious   101

Chapter 18 – The Answer Isn't In Thought   106

Chapter 19 – I Am   110

Chapter 20 – Dancing By Itself   113

Chapter 21 – A Center-less Center   119

Chapter 22 – Nothing Personal   127

Chapter 23 – My Song Is Silence   136

Chapter 24 – A Single Eye   138
Chapter 25 – Who Dies   141
Chapter 26 – A Love So Radiant   146
Chapter 27 – No Goal But This   149
Chapter 28 – No Place Like Home   152

This book is dedicated to Kathryn Comly.
I love you, Mom, beyond words.
There's just gratitude for you,
Beyond expression.

What you are the mind can never know. What you are produced the mind. How can that which is produced perceive its producer? The problem is, you think you are the mind. The perceived can never perceive the Perceiver – that which is Seeing. Not knowing its limits, the mind keeps trying to find its Source, to no avail.

Preface

One of my all-time favorite book titles is called, "The Lazy Man's Guide to Enlightenment," written in the early seventies by a man living in San Francisco named Thaddeus Golas. I was seven years old living on the opposite coast when it was published, but I didn't read it until about twenty years later. It was a decent little book and I remember enjoying it, but it lacked clear pointers to Truth – and gave you the impression that you, as a separate person, could become enlightened. Realizing it would be silly to write a book with the same title, I simply switched the word 'Guide' to 'Way' and added a subtitle. This book is filled with pointers to the Reality You Are, and it is my hope that you get a real sense of your True Identity – the Lazy Man's Way.

That's what this book is essentially about – who you REALLY are – because when you discover your true nature, everything else falls into place. Human beings are wired in such a way as to place attention on all the thoughts, sensations, feelings and experiences that come and go, instead of finding out what it is that is experiencing all of that. As a result of being focused on the 'outer world' of events, we often find ourselves tormented and confused by what happens to us. Not knowing who we really are, we invariably suffer. Granted, our lives have happy and joyous times, too, but pain and suffering is usually right around the corner.

The Reality is, there is an immense amount of benevolence in and around you – and nothing is excluded. Love, laughter and close relationships are enjoyed, and desires fulfilled, sometimes at the expense of our wellbeing. Having the good fortune of enjoying a summer home at the Jersey Shore with my parents and five siblings, I got to experience the beauty and magnificence of the Atlantic Ocean, spending much of my time surfing, body-surfing and boogey boarding. I felt so alive when I was riding those waves – and the bigger the better! Looking back, I didn't know that riding waves would later serve as a great metaphor for living in harmony with all of Life's waves of thought, sensation and experience.

I was pretty happy as a kid, excelled in athletics and was popular in school – you know, the things the ego deems important. As you may suspect, I derived a lot of my self-esteem from playing sports, but always sensed that I wasn't what I 'did' or excelled in. As I entered my late teens, I didn't feel that aliveness when I wasn't riding waves. Low self-esteem and depression set in, and I turned to drinking to alleviate the suffering. It became my strategy to numb the pain. On the wheel of suffering I went, and it lasted for a good fifteen years or more. When I stopped playing sports collegiately, I was lost. No longer could I identify with that guy who was good at a particular sport, and my life spiraled out of control.

And yet, amidst destructive behaviors, I usually had my nose in some self-help book because what I really wanted more than anything was simply to be happy. The methods followed never delivered on their promises, at least not long term. All methods live and function in time, and I was after the timeless. I wanted more than happiness, actually. I wanted freedom – freedom from my mind and emotions. I wanted happiness for no good reason. It took several more years of suffering until I realized that the key to happiness was in the discovery of my Real

Identity. Having been drawn to the terms 'liberation' and 'enlightenment,' I immersed myself in reading books on Eastern mysticism and enlightenment. In time, I would seek out enlightened teachers and sit in their presence.

Finally seeing that discovering my real nature *and* drinking alcohol would never work, I knew it had to go. Somehow Grace relieved me of the obsession to drink – and I haven't had a desire to drink in almost a decade and a half. It's not even a consideration to go back to the old ways. What bigger love could there be than the allowing of one to live out their destructive patterns and illusory beliefs, all the while having the opportunity to see through illusion to the animating Reality behind it all? Fear, anger, jealousy, insecurity and confusion was perfectly allowed to unfold as it did – and it seemed so real! I saw what I believed and believed what I saw. Everything was sustained and reinforced by this way of seeing…

What went unrecognized was what held all that, what breathed life into all that. What went unnoticed was what saw all that as divinely appropriate for this body/mind. You are that 'what' – not the Silent Witness, but the Silent, Witnessing Presence of Awareness that sees everything that arises with equanimity and affection, no matter what. You are a lover of what is, not a lover of what could or should be. Things can be falling apart all around you, but there is something within you that never falls apart. There can be big waves or little waves, turbulent times or peaceful times, but what happens at the surface can never affect the depths of the Heart. There could be a tsunami wreaking mass destruction and what you really are remains untouched by all of it. The appearances and experiences do not matter, no matter how seemingly frightening or undesired.

The welcoming capacity you are allows all of it in, and then watches in delight. You are the Author of the entire Play – the Ocean of Consciousness that has allowed itself to forget itself, in order to remember itself. It has forgotten that it, too, is the wave just as much as the ocean. And in this forgetting, You get to experience your Self, for if it were not for this forgetting, experiencing your Self couldn't happen. Clearly it's not an 'it' as it can never be an object in Awareness, for it is the Subject itself that gives rise to – and is none other than – all objects appearing. As you look deeply into the nature of Reality, relax that inner contraction, turning Awareness back on Itself – you may see that You are the ever-present space of knowing awareness that everything comes and goes in.

Falling into the silent and empty ground of being, prior to experience – and underlying all experience – you may get a taste of what's immediate and primary. Are You not always present before, during and after every thought, feeling, sound, sensation and experience, no matter how 'good' or 'bad?' Hasn't it been fun getting lost in all your temporal and passing creations of the mind, pretending that they can hurt You? Hasn't all the drama and struggle been fascinating – even addicting? How about the attachment to suffering? Hasn't that been a ride? But believing that there's something that can be apart from You has stolen the show, hasn't it? And now you want to give all that up to finally see who You are? Are you sure? After all, it's been so 'fun!' Simply forgetting Who You Are is all it took – and then pretending not to know there is no 'other' was a great formula for experiencing your Self, wasn't it? Forgetting that You are just as much the wave as the Ocean has led to all kinds of rip currents and eddies, hasn't it?

But it seems you've had enough. Thank goodness for the deep longing to come Home, for without it, there'd be no real spark to remember. Ultimately it doesn't matter, but apparently being identified with the body and mind is coming to an end. Okay, then. Start seeing. See what is present before, during and after each sensation, thought and experience. See what already deeply accepts everything as it is, before the mind starts to label and resist. See what never leaves. You are the Wordless

Reality that never comes and goes, the Space where all words appear and disappear. See that You don't ever come and go. See that You were present from the beginning – even before the beginning. And wake up to the dream, the lazy man's way.

Introduction

Most books about enlightenment and spirituality involve personal growth and becoming a better or higher version of you. The implication is that there is a greater goal to be attained, something that you haven't yet reached. They claim that all the Sages and Enlightened Masters have attained this state of being – and if you want what they have, then you have to make a journey in time towards becoming enlightened. This message speaks to the sense that something isn't right with you, and that you have to 'work on' yourself. It reinforces the belief that you are a separate entity living in the world, trying to make your life work.

The expectation is that in order to become enlightened, you must either purify yourself, become more spiritual or worthy enough to reach that elusive state primarily reserved for the extraordinary and chosen few. The way to enlightenment, they say, has to do with ridding yourself of 'unholy' thoughts and behaviors – and by clearing limiting patterns in the subconscious mind. Then, and only then, do 'you' have the chance of becoming enlightened. But until then, you're 'just not there yet.' In other words, get ready for a whole lot of effort if you desire the peace that surpasses all understanding.

The good news is that exercises or processes aren't needed to realize what you are. All that takes time – and you are Timeless. This isn't about gaining or improving anything; this is all about losing something, which takes no effort at all. These so-called teachers and gurus do a great disservice to those that earnestly seek to awaken to who (what) they really are. Steeped in a conceptual understanding of the nature of reality, these teachers suggest that you, as an individual, are capable of making choices and putting forth the effort required to reach Liberation – all the while sustaining and reinforcing the idea of seeking and becoming. As a result, you're told a progressive path towards a future state of enlightenment is required. And none of it is even remotely true.

In fact, this message almost assures that the discovery of what you are will remain elusive, when all along it is so radically simple and natural. We do not need to move elsewhere to discover Truth or Reality, for it is unconditionally present. Truth is simple, not complex. It is so immediately available and ordinary that it is overlooked – and it is so open that it seems hidden. It needs no path to trek. This book challenges the common assumption that you are a person who is reading this right now, and that you are a person who can 'do' something to reach a state called 'enlightenment.'

The reality is, enlightenment is beyond any notion of a 'you' that can achieve anything. It's beyond any notion of becoming or attaining a higher or better version of you. Enlightenment is right here, right now – and it *is* what you already are, regardless of whether it has been realized or not. Having a sense of being a separate individual is necessary in order to function in the world. If not for this sense, you wouldn't know which mouth to feed when you are hungry – or when to turn around when your name is called.

And yet, when it comes to awakening to your true nature, identifying who you are with your personality and body/mind only keeps the dream-state alive. This is about waking up *to* the dream. Your Real Identity is prior to the body/mind. Your Real Identity is that which the dream appears in. Thinking that the ego-personality can actually become enlightened is a deceptive way for the ego to postpone its own unmasking. It doesn't want to be seen for the phantom it is. Thinking that the personality can become enlightened is as futile as trying to bring your child a bucket of blue water from the sea to help him build an elaborate sandcastle. As much as you try, it just can't happen.

However, if we look in the direction where Liberation is waiting to be discovered, there's a possibility that a complete transformation can occur. Make no mistake about it: To awaken to what you are – and for Liberation to occur, a shift in perception must happen. And it's never merely conceptual, but it's *always* experiential. Paradoxically, it is not an experience, for all experiences have a beginning, middle and end. It is not a particular experience among other experiences, but the ground of all experience. Nonetheless, when it is seen what you really are, all doubt dissolves in the doubt-free Reality you are. It is self-authenticating and the proof is in the pudding. You know that you know, and nothing can ever obstruct this knowing.

If you focus on the meaning of the words in this book instead of what the words are pointing to, I can almost guarantee that this will just be another book about enlightenment that you can file away in the deep recesses of your mind. The words throughout are meant to go beyond belief, religion and philosophy, in order to stimulate a recognition and remembrance of what is already known. Words are dualistic by nature and can only describe something in terms of its opposite – and ultimately fail in attempting to describe the Non-dual nature of Reality. It is for this reason that you will undoubtedly encounter seeming contradictions and paradoxes throughout, particularly when pointing to This That You Really Are.

The point is this: you won't understand this with the mind, but what you really ARE understands this perfectly. You'll notice words like 'I,' 'me,' 'you,' 'we' and 'it' are used throughout. These words are mere concepts in the mind without ultimate reality – so the suggestion is not to conclude their use as contradictory. Words that are capitalized refer to the Ultimate Reality, the All-Inclusive Suchness of things – and aren't meant to exclude or divide. The capitalization is meant to emphasize the True Nature of the Infinite. The paragraphs are intentionally shorter as you may want to pause and look to where the words point. This isn't a teaching and I am not a teacher. Consider this as a sharing to remind You of what You already know.

And so, the invitation here is to drop all expectation – and everything you've accumulated up to this point, including all your spiritual notions and beliefs from any particular tradition, for the sake of another possibility that can transform everything. If you resist the urge to read this book looking for 'the answer,' you could begin to sense that which is beyond answers. You will also be invited to investigate and see if there actually is a seeker looking for enlightenment, truth, awakening, etc. You'll be encouraged to drop all conceptual knowledge for the purpose of discovering the non-conceptual Reality you are. When you discard all belief and opinion, and what others have told you – *and find out in your own direct experience* – you may get a taste of the essence of Reality beyond words.

Resting in the space of awareness that is prior to all conceptualization, you may *see* much more than a taste. But remember this: you won't 'get' anything here for there is nothing to get. Clearly, this is about losing something. There is nothing of real significance here for the mind to chew on, so you can let the mind do its thing. In fact, you won't find much food for the mind here. You are, as you are, a divine expression – before any conceptualization.

Don't expect this to be logical and reasonable; this is anything but logical and reasonable. The truth is, there is absolutely nothing wrong with you and there is absolutely nothing that needs to be worked through or changed in order to see what you've always been. Leave the mind be.

There is nowhere to go, and nothing to accomplish. All you need 'do' is simply recognize you already are that which you seek.

David A. Bhodan
October – 2012

Chapter 1
A Case of Mistaken Identity

"When I observe myself, I am really forced to admit that every day I am a prisoner of a thousand unsatisfied desires, or desires whose satisfaction brings me no permanent bliss. So it seems to me that instead of endless running from one desire to another, it would be better to stop and examine the true nature of desire. If this investigation is successful, you will penetrate the nature of the true aim of all desire. What any desire really aims at, is a state of non-desire."

– Jean Klein

When I don't know what I am, I am often left unsettled. When I don't know what I am, I am forever subject to the "slings and arrows of outrageous misfortune," cycling in and out of resistance, pain and confusion.

You've probably read (or sense) that you aren't who you take yourself to be, but when you read or sense that, what do you generally do? Do you dismiss it and move to the next thing that captures your attention?

Or do you really deeply look into who and what you are?

No really, do you?

1

When we talk about ourselves, we generally talk about the story of who we are, and the story our mind tells about our identity. We say, "I am a man, fifty-three years old, a successful entrepreneur, a devout Christian with a loving wife and four children." Or "I am a forty year old white woman, a Buddhist, a good person and caring wife and mother."

We give a brief description of our autobiography based on past events and experiences, both happy and sad, sprinkling in future hopes, desires and aspirations.

However, you are not the story of your race, your income level, or religious affiliation. You are not your past or future successes or failures, sexual orientation and intellectual capacity. You are not your happy or sad childhood. In fact, you aren't any "thing" at all. You are none of these "things."

What you really are cannot be explained or defined. What you really are has no name or form, either.

All the authentic spiritual teachers, sages and mystics have been reminding us that in reality, you are not the separate person you appear to be, but the immense ocean of consciousness in which every manifest wave of thought, sensation and experience appears and disappears in. You are the timeless and space-less capacity for all of life to unfold, including the appearance of a separate person.

This non-separateness of the self and world is ultimately what all the spiritual teachings and religions point to, and this inseparability is now being confirmed by science. Modern science has proven that nothing is separate – and that each and every particle is part and parcel to everything else. Everyone knows this, but has simply forgotten.

You are Life itself.

Underneath the roles we play as mothers, fathers, wives, husbands, brothers, sisters, friends, teachers, students, business owners, employees, etc., is our True Identity. Like waves in the ocean of life, we may have different shapes and sizes. We may have different roles, beliefs, conditioning, opinions, skills and abilities.

And while we may be unique expressions in the ocean of consciousness, our Real Essence is exactly the same.

Our Real Essence doesn't differ, not even a little bit.

Oneness doesn't preclude diversity; Oneness gives birth to diversity.

Before you know anything, you *are* everything.

As young children, there is simply being, without a knowing of being. And then someone comes along and gives you a name and calls you 'Joe' or 'Kay' – and tells you that you're a 'person' living in this world. And the goal is to be successful, healthy and happy.

All the while, the entire investment is in "I am a person and I'm here to make my life work." Somehow, the mind usurps and takes ownership of the energy of being and identifies with the "I" thought – and *becomes* Joe or Kay.

And it's just a mental image, an imagined self-center with no independent existence.

The mind hijacks Being (in reality, it can't) and gives it a name. The use of language and labels start to form, and the whole notion of "me" becomes the primary investment of living.

From here on out, absolutely everything that happens is referenced back to this "me" of memory – the "me" that is apparently separate from all the other "me's" with names and forms. All the while, True Identity is beyond name and form. As all the mystics say, your True Identity is nameless and formless.

Identified with the mind, I naturally avoid pain and seek pleasure. Invariably, my energy and attention is focused on defending the current image I have of myself. It doesn't always work, but that's what I am inclined to do. Little do I realize that an image isn't real; little do I see that I'm looking in the wrong direction.

The root of all seeking is a belief in separation.

This is also the birth of suffering. While it is natural and functional to have a sense of being a separate self, we erroneously make the leap and conclude it means we *must be* a separate self. And so our life goes.

In reality, it is simply the One Being playing the game of being "other," in order to remember there is no other. It is the One Being allowing itself to forget itself, in order to play the game of pretending to be an individual.

So, let me ask you. Who do you think you are? Who are you REALLY? Are you that person staring back in the mirror? Is what you see in the mirror the same thing as what is peering through those eyes at the mirror? What I am looking out of is different from what I am looking at in the mirror.

Douglass Harding said, *"When I look in the mirror, that is what I am looking at, but what I am looking out of is Space. I appear to be a solid lump, but here I am transparent: it is a total difference, in every respect."*

What is already effortlessly aware of present sights and sounds? What is already effortlessly aware of thoughts, sensations and feelings? What is already aware of beliefs and opinions?

You are not your thoughts or beliefs, for you are aware of them. You are not any feeling or sensation, for you are of aware of them. You aren't any objects you see for you are aware of them, too.

Something in you is aware of all these 'things.' What is conscious of everything? What is fully present always? What is that? What notices everything coming and going?

Whatever you can know about your 'self' is an object and therefore, isn't it. Whatever you can see, think and feel about your 'self' are also objects and therefore, isn't it, either. What can be seen, felt or known isn't it. Ego is a perceived object, and not the perceiving awareness. What is doing the seeing is Aware Spirit, which all objects seen appear in.

Mistakenly identified with what can be seen, felt and known, we have confused what we are with objects in perception, and not that which is doing the perceiving. An ego personality is an object and isn't what you really are. If it can be noticed, it can't be what you are.

4

Are you your mind and body – or do you have a mind and body?

Are you a man or a woman of a certain age and background with a particular family history, education level and career path? Are you your self-image of yourself? Can you be an image?

Is your True Identity really a "mother," "father," "son," "daughter," "sister" or "brother?" Can you *be* the role you play?

Are you your thoughts about yourself? If you are aware of the thoughts you have about yourself, how could you *be* those thoughts?

Wouldn't you have to be prior in order to notice the thoughts?

How do you define who you are? Are you a person that changes, has good and bad experiences, and grows old and dies? Are you the running story you've identified with that seems to change according to the circumstances in "your" life?

Are you really a separate, limited individual existing independently amongst six and half other billion people? Do you really and truly have a birth date and a day you will surely die? Have you ever really looked deeply into this?

Can you honestly say that there is anything more important than finding out who you Really are? Wouldn't everything else, especially the quality and experience of life hinge on knowing this?

Wouldn't it?

Does it make sense to find out who you believe you are right now, in order to find out, beyond belief, what you really are? Don't most of us believe we were created on a particular date in time, born of two parents, given a name, live for a particular time period, experience the full gamut of highs and lows, and then perish like so many before?

In other words, one day we weren't even a glimmer in our parents eyes and then poof, here we are? Like a magician pulling a rabbit out of his hat, out of seeming nowhere, here you are, possessing a body and mind with preferences, needs, desires, interests, abilities and weaknesses – *none of which you chose.*

Do you believe yourself to be someone at a certain point in your life trying to get to another higher or better point in the future? Aren't you the central character in the story of your life – and that every experience impacts who you are, positively or negatively?

When your body breathes its last breath, do you believe you cease with it? Or do you have a belief that you go to heaven as a reward for treating others well and/or following a certain creed – and maybe a place called 'hell' or 'purgatory' if you didn't?

Most of us live out our entire lives not knowing who we really are, dismissing the significance of it to the background of our awareness. Only when we deeply inquire into our beliefs and assumptions about who we think we are, do we remotely give ourselves the chance to really *see* what we are.

The mind may make it complex, but in actuality, it's fairly simple to recognize and know what you really are because what you really are never changes. It's always right here, within present experience – and it can be confirmed in your actual experience.

Is it possible that you might really be the Changeless Reality that all change happens within?

Might you be the aware presence that doesn't come and go?

Could you be the Light that illuminates everything equally, without bias or preference?

No one is implying you must want or need to know what you are. The good news is you can live as you wish. You can even believe you are the Easter Bunny or The Tooth Fairy if you want.

Heck, as a kid, I pretended to be Ultra-man and Spiderman for a while, until I saw that I couldn't climb walls or fly straight up into space when I needed energizing. When I got proof I wasn't either, I couldn't pretend anymore. Ultimately, it doesn't really matter; you can only really be what you already are.

Nevertheless, if we no longer wish to experience an identity crisis, then the direction is towards simplicity and not complexity. Isn't that nice to know? You don't need high intelligence or superior abilities, either. In fact, the intellect often gets in the way of this seeing. And you certainly don't need to be special.

How fortunate for this author!

But if we allow our beliefs about ourselves to go unquestioned, and if we naively follow what others tell us, we can be sure most of us have unnecessary drama and a good amount of inner division in our future – a future, by the way, that doesn't exist other than in our minds.

If we take ourselves to be a separate individual living for a certain number of years, only to end up taking the proverbial dirt nap, we're forever mistaking ourselves to *be* our body/mind. With that identification comes a natural inclination to avoid pain and gain pleasure, a surefire recipe for *more* pain and less pleasure.

I don't need to know you in order to know you are seeking wholeness and completeness. It comes with the package. It's a natural impulse all humans share. We can name it 'Enlightenment,' 'Awakening,' 'Liberation' or 'Freedom.' It doesn't matter. The word isn't the thing.

Concepts can never capture Reality.

No one wants to feel alienated, empty and lonely. In our spiritual poverty, we go to great lengths to avoid feeling inadequate, unhappy and isolated. Well, most do. Some people are quite content in their misery, or as Pink Floyd would say, "comfortably numb."

When we forget our essential inseparability from Life itself, and identify as the limited time-bound image of 'me,' we feel homesick, seemingly far from the One we are. And then the search begins. We seek that One in time – seeking respect, fortune, love, enlightenment, or whatever we think will deliver us home.

All the while, we're looking *from* Home. All the while, we never left Home.

We distract ourselves in a variety of ways, buying 'stuff' ranging from cars, homes, clothes and a whole host of other "things" in an attempt to mask the perceived void felt inside – that seeming hole that can't ever be filled by things external to us. The truth is, there isn't a hole inside, and there isn't anything external. It just feels that way.

The bottomless bowl of separation only intensifies the longing for Wholeness we presume we've lost. Stuck in misidentification, we go round and round until we don't anymore. We may become utterly exhausted from the search and give up. It is in this giving up that a new possibility can be revealed.

Misperception and illusion have that kind of power. Because we perceive we're lacking in so many areas, we believe there is something missing, something not quite right. And what we perceive, we receive.

And it *all* stems from a case of mistaken identity. Fortunately, once you see what you really are, beyond any doubt, the identity crisis collapses and laughter and great relief ensues.

Before that, everything is referred to this reference point you call "you," isn't it? Understand that all problems arise from a belief in the idea of a separate "me" that must bring about a sense of alienation and confusion.

This unquestioned belief in separation is the cause of all your problems.

Hence, the underlying cause is the belief in a "me" independent of other "me's" – and the effects are "my" unhappiness, "my" anxiety, "my" fear and "my" anger. As a result, we set out to become happier, more balanced, more courageous and more peaceful, further cementing the endless illusory cycle we're trapped in.

All because we don't know who we are.

To be free of suffering, all we need do is look and see if there is anyone here separate from anything at all, including the world that is perceived with our limited senses. Looking beyond appearances, what do we find? If we don't look, we firmly believe, without investigation, that we *are* the ego personality, separate from other personalities living *in* this world.

The word "ego" is casually tossed around as if it's real. Ego is simply the movement of thought, which we call thinking. In other words, there is no entity called an "ego" we can locate. When we investigate for ourselves, we can't locate this "me." Where is it? Look like you've never looked before – and please, take as long as you wish.

Where is this reference point you call "me?" Is it possible it's just a thought?

If the cause is seen to be false, what must happen to the effects? Without a cause, there can't be any effects. Seen through, they must drop away. Find out what you truly are and the ballgame is over – and a whole new adventure begins.

From a sense of lack, a sense that something is missing, the search for wholeness and fulfillment ensues, further reinforcing our sense of separation. But what if the void we seek to fill is already full? What if we already *are* the living fulfillment, in its entirety, before we go in search of it?

What if the wholeness and peace we seek is already fully present, contained in every aspect of experience – and all that appears in our experience? What if who you really are was never an individual person living in this world, but the open space of welcoming awareness in which the *appearance of an individual* appears in?

What if who you are is already unconditionally, inextricably free and at peace?

What if what you really are fully embraces every thought, sensation and experience as it is – without a need to change any of it? What if all that you avoid and deem undesirable is fully welcomed and inseparable from the One you really are?

And what if this embrace has already happened and will continue to happen, prior to you seeking it? Recognizing this, what journey to wholeness or enlightenment would you need to take? Wouldn't it already be the case? Wouldn't it then just become a matter of recognizing what is already so?

Wouldn't it render everything absolutely perfect as it is – even the things you used to deem imperfect?

Are you ready to discover what you REALLY are?

Are you ready to *then live* the implications of this discovery?

Chapter 2
Lost in Translation

"The words of Truth are always paradoxical."

– Lao Tzu

The thought of a chair isn't the actual chair. The thought of enlighten-ment isn't actual enlightenment. Additionally, the word is never the thing. Can you drink the word, "milk?" Can you eat the word, "cookie?"

The words in this book won't ever succeed in describing what you are, what truth or reality is – but we'll give it a go. The best that words can do to describe Truth or Reality is to invite you to look within – and see what the words are pointing to.

No matter how clever the use of words, they can never logically resolve the Great Paradox for you. And nothing in your mind will ever become enlightened. The mind doesn't wake up. You wake up *to* the mind. And then it doesn't matter what the mind asserts – ever.

Inherent in the use of words to describe something lies a sense of separation. When I explain something, implied in that description is what it is not. Language divides and separates that which isn't divided and separate.

Labels, descriptions and definitions are boundaries; they are mental divisions created in the mind, where in Reality there aren't any. The mind's function is to compartmentalize that which is boundless.

And since our language is a language of boundaries, it makes it difficult to point to This That You Are. In describing anything, we're simultaneously erecting a seeming boundary with it, and everything unlike it. We say, "Everything that doesn't look like a bird or a tree *isn't* a bird or a tree."

In order to communicate, convey and understand, language starts to take place early on. Babies learn different concepts like, "Momma," "Dadda," and "blankie." However, the word "Momma" and "Dadda" aren't actually Momma and Dadda. The word "blankie" isn't the actual blanket.

In their true purpose and function, words are meant to help translate the word to the actual, but we often forget the word can never be the thing.

We're all aware that it takes years to learn the various labels for existence, and that it takes even longer to put them all together in a cohesive way that makes sense for us.

Words have no inherent meaning; they are simply sounds and symbols pointing to the variety of life's happenings. For example, one happening is called "rain," another is called "happiness" and another is called "believing."

In a different language, these three concepts would have no meaning at all to the translator. They'd be merely sounds signifying nothing at all. If you were Swahili, the words "rain," "happiness" and "believing" would be total nonsense. The point is this: words have no basic meaning at all.

Even words like "rain," "happiness" and "believing" have no intrinsic meaning, even to those who understand English. We live in realms of linguistic fabrication, interpreting concepts based on familiar patterns of recognition from the past and what makes sense to us at the time.

Similarly, the word "God," "Truth" or "Reality" isn't God, Truth or Reality. The word "God" isn't God, is it? The word "Truth" isn't the actual Truth, is it? The word "God" is such a highly charged word, with as many different meanings as there are those who utter the word.

We maim and kill over the interpretation of "our" God.

Do you think the word is the actual? If so, the next time you're thirsty, go have a sip of the word "water" and see if it quenches your thirst. When you're hiking in the woods and stop to camp out on a chilly night, try to warm up with the word "fire" and see if you get warm.

When we mistake words for the actual, we unwittingly lie to ourselves. We deceive ourselves without ever realizing it – and we do it often. In a trance-like state, rarely do we question whether the words we use are anything but a fiction. Fictions are illusory – and illusion hurts. Have you noticed?

It's plain and simple; words only point.

None of us come out of they womb saying, "Hey, it's about time I got out of there, can I get some milk?" Babies have no concepts or ideas, nor do they make distinctions and judge. They are simply being, crying when moved to cry, wetting when moved to wet, eating when moved to eat, and sleeping when moved to sleep.

It may finally dawn on us that the question for the translator is not just the use and function of language, but its validity and truthfulness. Believing in appearances as the Reality without seeing beyond to the Singular, animating Essence, a sense of separation abounds.

Separation brings pain. Believing I am separate from all existence, suffering must arise.

There is nothing separate from Oneness needing to find Oneness.

But if it's Truth or Reality we're after, seeing through the limits of words and labels is requisite. Seeing the true function of language is requisite. Transcending the limits of language in order to *see* what's actually happening in this, timeless moment – and not what the mind is telling us about what's happening – is requisite.

Mere words lay on the surface, yet point to something underneath. Hanging out at the surface, it never gets seen that the essence underneath is waiting to be discovered. Words barely scratch the surface, yet we spend a lifetime scratching at the surface, thinking we can arrive at the essence underneath.

On the occasion we go below the surface, we allow for the opportunity for something to finally "click" – and we *see* what the word is pointing to. We notice the essence of a pointer – and that which it points to isn't in the word. We can appreciate the pointer for what it is and notice that it's in the accurate non-conceptual translation of the word, that which the word is pointing to.

As the ancient Buddhist saying goes, *"Concepts are like fingers pointing to the moon, so don't mistake the finger for the moon itself."*

We are wise not to get caught up looking at the finger and completely miss out on the brilliance of the moon.

Whenever we find ourselves confused or in doubt, it's a good indicator we're stuck on the concept, instead of looking to where the concept is pointing.

The heart of the matter here is simply (and effortlessly) recognizing what's already so – and remembering what you really are, non-conceptually. You are prior to, and beyond the formation of words and concepts.

Before words, you are.

Words don't happen *to* you; they happen *within* you, forever coming and going in the unchanging awareness you are.

Nevertheless, here are more inadequate, contradictory, paradoxical and unnecessary words for you. Don't get hung up on a single one. Using words, however inadequate, let us go beyond the words to which they point.

Don't get stuck looking at the finger that you completely miss out on that which it is pointing to.

Chapter 3
The Price of Admission

"Knowledge is knowing that we cannot know."
– Ralph Waldo Emerson

Can you admit to yourself that perhaps you really don't know what you are? Can you admit to yourself that maybe all your beliefs, assumptions and opinions you have about yourself and God might simply just be that – beliefs, assumptions and opinions?

Can you acknowledge the fear and discomfort at the thought of letting all your beliefs, assumptions and opinions go? Can you acknowledge the potential difficulty in letting go of your entire investment in your God?

If you can, can you then meet that fear and discomfort without trying to alter it?

Paradoxically, the reality is that only when you allow yourself *not* to know, do you give yourself the opportunity *to* know.

Life lived without a purpose or agenda frightens the mind that must have a direction in life. The last thing we want is to not know where we're headed. After all, those who fail to plan, plan to fail.

Without a concrete purpose, position and direction, who would we be? What would we do? How would we feel about ourselves? What would others think of us? Would we lose all drive and motivation? We can't even count how many attachments we have to *things* we can't imagine living without.

We're taught from a young age that to "get" anywhere in life – and in order to be happy, we must get a good education, get a good job making good money, and meet the "right" person, perhaps settling down and having a family.

What is your definition of failure? How do you define success? Are both relative to what you achieve and collect in this short life? Are you your successes and failures? If you came to the end of your life – and you weren't overly productive and didn't achieve a whole lot, how would you feel?

Since tomorrow isn't guaranteed, what if today was your last day?

So much of our esteem and identity is wrapped up in where we've been, where we are, what we've achieved, and where we plan to be some day. When a future self is imagined, it's always a present experience. When a past self is remembered, it's always a present experience.

It's always now. Past and future "selves" are merely concepts in the mind, without any reality at all – and yet these imaginings have a tendency to torture us until we see them for what they really are – simply arbitrary and imagined criteria to meet in order to feel good about who we think we are.

The notion of simply resting in what is (Reality is what is) brings up all kinds of awkward sensations we'd rather not experience. However, when we can recognize that the mind naturally resists what is, we are that much closer to waking up to what we are.

And yet, it can happen *right now*. It is *that* available and immediate.

If sensations are already happening, resisting what's already happening isn't the most rational and sane thing to do, is it? Can any present happening be any different than it is? Despite what the mind says, no, it cannot.

To complicate matters, we're so emotionally invested in our beliefs about everything under the sun. The thought of giving up anything, including who it is we think we are, who our God is, and where we think we're headed in the afterlife is very uncomfortable to say the least.

It is a scary proposition, indeed, especially when we think we *are* the mind.

That's why so few are ready to hear this message. Incidentally, this message isn't for your mind. In fact, this entire book's message isn't for your mind. It is for You, that which mind arises and dissolves in.

So few are ready to hear there isn't an afterlife, because there isn't a before life. Afterlife implies time when there isn't any. Life, what you are, is eternal and always outside the stream of time. Life is timeless.

Instead of worrying about an afterlife, wouldn't it make sense to find out what you are now?

Reality is without a beginning, middle or end. If it had a beginning, middle and an end, it would have to be an experience. All experience is temporal and happens within Reality. This has nothing to do with any experiential quality. What you are is not an experience. What you are is beyond the senses.

What you are is the Space where all experience happens within.

Most ego-personalities cling to the concept of an afterlife in an attempt to ensure its survival after the body dies. It wants the comfort and security thinking it's going somewhere after physical death. Funny thing is, ego (the mind) does die with the body. So the thing you desire to continue on after the body dies is toast! In fact, it never existed in the first place. What a waste of energy, isn't it?

What you are never dies because what you are was never born. You are prior to the cycle of birth and death. The cycle of birth and death arise in what you are.

Our attachments are basically emotional patterns of energy that seem so solid that it becomes to define who and what we are. They become reference points lived from, rather than opportunities to see we aren't those attachments and patterns of energy.

It's our emotional bond with things, beliefs and assumptions that need to be looked at and severed in order to awaken to what we truly are.

Come as you are. The price of admission is being unreservedly willing to let absolutely everything go, including everything we deem most important. We no longer cling to anything, knowing what we cling to we're bound by.

As Jesus said, *"Unless you become like a little child, you will never enter the Kingdom of Heaven."* You must enter completely naked.

The price of admission is all about a loss – a profound loss that believe it or not, you won't miss or regret losing.

Until your life is lost, you'll always seek.

It's a stripping away of all the false ideas – especially the existence of time and being an individual. Like a ball of twine unraveled, nothing is left but a timeless, awake, aware, empty space of knowing where everything appears and disappears in.

That's what you are; timeless, changeless empty being – yet full of the changing, passing scene. Being open to the real possibility that there is no "you" living a life, but that Life is living itself through you, as you, is the ticket that buys your entry.

And yet, there is no entry. There is no "you" to enter anything because there's no "you" that left.

Although it may feel as if there is something to enter, as in a door or a gate, there isn't anything to enter. Upon the seeing of what you are, you turn back and notice there never was a door or gate to enter through. Like everything else, it was just an imagined concept.

In Zen, they call this the "gateless-gate."

So, are you ready to lose your entire world? Losing your entire world for the sake of gaining the whole world is requisite. As Jesus said, *"Die before you die."* What he was pointing to was the death of the "you" you think you are.

We don't have the luxury of holding onto *any* of it (including our cherished false sense of security fashioned by belief) if we desire the freedom that liberates.

In a world where absolutely everything is transient, clinging to what's inherently impermanent must bring suffering. In an open state of discovery, an honest and uncompromising inquiry into everything we believe ourselves to be – and who we take ourselves to be is needed.

In truth, even inquiry isn't really needed. Who is there present *to* inquire? Who is present to lose or need anything? However, it can still be useful.

What can't be gained can never be truly lost.

The discovery of truth is in the discernment of the false. Peel away all that is untrue and what remains is true. Like an onion, what is left when you peel away all the layers? Just pure empty space, that's all. But different than a peeled onion, This space is empty, knowing and aware.

A deep wonder and curiosity is our orientation if we want to know what we are. When we know what we are, we know what Reality is. The longing to know what God is, is essentially a longing to know what you are, for when you discover what you are, you discover what God is.

Realization does not come from personal effort, belief or any quality of thinking. When we allow what is to be as it is, we give ourselves the opportunity to transcend dualism, at the same including dualism. Seeing beyond belief and dualism, our limited senses are transcended – and it is seen that all arises in the non-dual Awareness that everything is dependent on.

Overlooking the ever-present and necessary awareness prior to all content and deeming it insignificant, you don't see that without it, nothing is. Nothing can stand independent of the awareness that perceives it. And in this overlooking, you completely miss out on the discovery of what you are really are.

All the while, "it is closer than breathing, nearer than hands and feet."

Understanding and embracing paradoxes (and seeming contradictions inherent in language), clarity replaces confusion. Clarity, or clear seeing, requires no special qualifications or degrees. No chanting, lighting incense or getting into the lotus position to meditate is needed to see and be what you already are.

Let go of all expectations and demands. Expectations and demands presumes – and Reality doesn't. Come innocent and pure. Give up your habitual attachment to struggle and effort for the sake of directly experiencing the peace beyond understanding, the joy without cause you are.

You are prior to all mental constructions at the same time allowing all mental constructions. You are the un-construct that allows all construction. You have no real life story; your apparent individual story is allowed in what you really are.

Self-knowledge is simply investigating, like a scientist, into the ideas and notions about what you believe yourself to be, and allowing for the possibility that none of it is true, now or ever.

Emptied of all notions, consider that all along, you've been whole and complete, never lacking a thing. Consider the possibility who you really are has never been a limited, finite being with a certain life span, here to live for a while only to die.

What you really long for and fear at the same time is the absence of you. The absence of the "you" is the presence of You. Why else do you think so many run to the movies, read book after book, play video games and watch TV so much? It's a nice distraction and brief respite from "you," isn't it?

Enlightenment is the absence of the 'you' you think you are. In this absence is a presence so wonderfully full and engaged, yet wholly unconcerned. The mind cannot fathom this; the mind can only imagine such a state of unconcern.

Look deeply into the idea that you are a separate entity navigating as best as "you" can, treading safely (or adventurously) to "your" eventual demise.

Consider the possibility that Life is complete as it is, and that within each moment, Reality is infinitely manifesting. All the apparent parts are nothing other than an expression of one magnificent Whole – and You Are That.

See that absolutely NONE of this takes any effort whatsoever. What effort is needed to arrive at the effortless? What journey is needed to arrive right here, right now – where you've always been? There is no preparation for now. How can there be preparation for the timeless?

In the end, the price of admission is the clear recognition that nobody ever needed admittance or preparation.

In the end, what is realized is that Liberation is a total poverty, a total loss of *everything*. Liberation is a total loss of individuality and separation – and belief in *anything* the mind comes up with, so that nothing but what you are remains.

This is what Christ was referring to when he said it is more difficult for a rich man to enter the kingdom of heaven than for a camel to pass through the eye of a needle.

When all is lost, and when you empty yourself, there is just fullness. When there is nothing left, there is just completeness, wholeness.

So come bare-naked, without the garments of your preconceived notions, beliefs or expectations. Drop anything you think you know; lay down anything you think you own, including your suffering. There isn't anyone who owns suffering. Pain and suffering happens within what you are.

Knock and the door shall be opened.

Chapter 4
Enlightenment Isn't What You Think

"Enlightenment is ego's ultimate disappointment."

– Chogyam Trungpa

I should warn you that I'm not an enlightened person – and you won't ever become enlightened, either. In fact, no one has ever been enlightened. There is no such thing as an "enlightened person." It is a contradiction in terms.

Awareness is all there is. You are Awareness Itself, not somebody who is aware. Enlightenment is rather simple. It's really nothing more than remembering something forgotten. It is nothing more, or other than, the realization of the true nature of Reality.

The definition of Reality is that which never changes.

See this.

YOU are that Reality, absolutely and completely as you are. Seeing this is the entire aim of this book.

Liberation is the spontaneous cognition and remembrance that separation and individuality are both illusory. Enlightenment knows the mind is an object in awareness, an appearance on the screen of the

23

Changeless Reality you are.

Enlightenment is the absence of any separate individual entity we call a person. Therefore, no one becomes enlightened. If anyone proclaims to be enlightened, simply nod your head and walk the other way.

Being what you are, it can't be learned, taught, given, taken away or lost.

And it has nothing to do with you or me.

Although it's so open and immediately available right where you are, as long as you try to "get it," it stays hidden.

And it's not a state of mind, and it is not an experience. It has absolutely nothing to do with mystical experiences or bliss. It's not about a special state of being, but it has everything to do with the natural state of being.

Typically, those who tend to gravitate towards the need to take on the role of "spiritual teacher" or "guru" attract those that need to take on the role of students. Coming from a spiritual ego in the guise of an "enlightened" person, the illusion of separation solidifies and continues.

The underlying message is, "I'm enlightened and you aren't, so you need to hear what I have to say if you want what I have." Subsequently, a divide is created, however subtle or significant, between the teacher and the student. Thus, the student aspires to be just like the teacher put up on a pedestal and perceived as "other."

All the while, there isn't any divide present but in the minds of those who believe one exists. All the while, the teacher's presence is the student's presence, without difference. No one owns or possesses more truth than another. Enlightenment simply is – and it's right now. It never needs to be attained or achieved, nor can it be.

It's so simple it utterly confounds the mind.

As we mentioned before, in truth, the word 'enlightenment' is just a concept that points to something else. Words are pointers only. The concept 'enlightenment' points to an actual and direct recognition there is no one present to need, attain or achieve anything – including enlightenment.

It is the absolute and complete absence of the one who is concerned about *being* enlightened. It is the Absolute aware of itself, manifesting as all appearance, in time and space.

There isn't anything for the ego in enlightenment. This is why most aren't ready for this radical message, precisely *because* there is nothing for sale. There's nothing to 'get' or 'possess.' Most are only ready for a message that makes sense to the mind – and this makes no sense at all to the mind.

After reading this book, most will go back to looking for something they can 'know' and 'do' – something that involves effort towards becoming something more, better or different. Some will file this away as hogwash, claiming that it just can't be this simple.

While it is so simple, ordinary and ever-present, it isn't so easy to recognize.

Enlightenment sees whatever is arising as it is, without conceptualization or preference. It has no need or desire to improve upon or avoid anything. It is equally content with the mundane as much as the extraordinary.

Minds love – and are drawn to, ideas of extraordinary powers, abilities and ways of being. Minds aren't particularly interested in "what is, as it is" because there's nothing really special about what is. Clouds tend to draw more attention than the empty sky. Minds want the noisy, glowing fireworks!

The mind only understands the rational, logical and linear – and this is anything but that. Minds are interested in (and can only understand) progressive paths, processes and journeys towards becoming something other, or more, than it already is.

And the mind can only comprehend that which is in time. Enlightenment is outside of time, prior to time.

A good friend of mine once said of enlightenment: *Enlightenment is when there is no longer an argument with yourself, others and the world.*

But by no means is this the only way to point towards enlightenment. In the end, enlightenment is just a fancy word we've been told to believe is mostly for the chosen few or special.

We've been taught it's for those who renounce everything and devote their entire life to seeking it, perhaps meditating in a cave for years until "it" apparently happens. The funny thing is, if you seek it you won't ever find it, for you are already enlightened. You just don't recognize it yet.

No caves, monasteries or trips to India are needed.

It is instantly available all the time, wherever you are. It is closer than breathing, in fact.

You can't know what it is either, nor *can* you know. However, once you recognize you already are it, you're Home – even though you never left Home. The search for enlightenment is essentially a desire to be whole and complete, when all the while you've never been less than whole and complete.

Like Dorothy clicking her heels to return to Kansas, you've always been in Kansas, but simply dreamed you weren't in Kansas. In order to awaken from the dream of individuality, it helps if you desire, "No place like home."

Those who have fully comprehended the nature of Reality without a shred a doubt, know that division and boundaries are mere mental constructs created in the mind – and are therefore unreal.

Reality is undivided and boundless, and *is* what you are. Sharing this with others need never be exaggerated, embellished or adorned, for that would be too much. It is so ordinary and without the bells and whistles that it is beyond comprehension. It is so much less than the mind could ever imagine – and it can never *be* what the mind imagines.

It is never what you think it is, because it can't be what you think it is. Thought can never approach it or box it up.

In fact, it is better to have no thought of enlightenment at all.

It's so devastatingly simple that to convey it with any special bells and whistles is not only inappropriate, but unnecessary, too. While most would assume it's a really cool state of being where bliss and ecstasy abound, it is actually rather ordinary and very natural.

In fact, it is your natural state of being, no matter what you think.

Granted, the implications are tremendous and immeasurable – and moments of bliss and ecstasy certainly do arise, but for no one.

Despite what many may imagine, it doesn't point to a permanent state of happiness or an eternal sense of being beyond human pain and drama. The primary difference is there is no longer identification with being a particular body-mind, apart from other body-minds. Having no reference point, things like pain and discomfort don't hang around long.

It doesn't mean things aren't felt. They are, but without the illusory idea of a separate entity experiencing it. Paradoxically, things are often felt deeper and more intensely – and without resistance. And since there isn't any ownership of the feelings, there's an intimacy felt, where before there was distance and denial.

Passing through like inclement weather below a sun so radiant, what you really are remains unaffected. Even when it's cloudy out, the sun is always shining.

And it's not simply a conceptual strategy to alleviate the painful sensations felt. It's not about forming a mental conclusion that says, "Oh, this doesn't really bother me because I know what I am – and I am beyond all that." This mental conclusion can only bring doubt and more unwanted insecurity.

I used to think that peace and surrender was something I had to "do" – and that they were states I could reach. However, what was discovered was that peace and surrender were already present before I went in search of it. They were both present realities that went overlooked. The knowing or 'seeing' of this *is* the peace that surpasses all understanding.

The amazing paradox is that there is nobody here separate from this moment that *can* surrender to this moment, and yet, a deep surrender of this moment is already occurring. All thought, sensation, sound and experience are already being allowed in the impartial Space that you are.

Peace and love are both present moment realities, aspects of what you really are, never needing to be attained or acquired. Seeking peace and love is to deny its presence. Before we seek peace and love, we can simply notice if it's not already present.

There's always an abiding sense that all is well, even if it doesn't appear that way. A deep and tangible peace is still felt, regardless of what's happening on the periphery. At least this is this author's experience.

In the Light of recognition, old patterns of thinking and behaving drop away. If inner division arises, it is seen through and usually discarded quickly – by no one. If pain occurs, resistance to the pain doesn't happen, nor does ownership of the pain happen. Pain comes up for a bit, expresses itself, and then leaves.

When pain is allowed to be as it is, suffering doesn't arise.

Enlightenment sees no separation or division anywhere, no good and bad, right and wrong or this and that. It is beyond the play of opposites while including them. It includes everything as equally appropriate, especially the things the mind deems *most* inappropriate.

Enlightenment is the realization that Life is unfolding as it is – and cannot unfold any other way, regardless of what the mind has to say. As the late Jesuit priest Anthony de Mello once said, *"Enlightenment is the absolute cooperation with the inevitable."*

If enlightenment could ever be described in terms of qualities, I see them as uncaused joy, compassion, deep humility and unconditional love. Rather than expressing these qualities, enlightenment points to Being as the essence of these qualities.

You're already that which you seek.

You can only *be* what you are; you cannot know what you are. The Subject, what you are, can never be known for it would have to be an object. Only an object can be known. You can only know what is not. What is – you can only be.

Whatever you think it is, that's not it. It is different from that.

Enlightenment, eternally beyond thought, can never be what you think.

Chapter 5
Belief Drops Away

"What is true is already so. Owning up to it doesn't make it worse. Not being open about it doesn't make it go away. And because it's true, it is what is there to be interacted with. Anything untrue isn't there to be lived. People can stand what is true, for they are already enduring it."

– Eugene Gendlin

I can tell you what I believe the color of the sky and the ocean is, but is it really true for you? I can tell you what I believe Truth is, what God is, and what the world around you is. I can even recite passages from the greatest mystics throughout the ages that are commonly viewed as enlightened and free.

I can present you evidence with mind blowing logic and reason, even claim it to be "historically recorded fact" until you are unequivocally convinced and prepared to give your life for the cause, but it will still only be belief for you, a misperception of Truth.

And since it may *feel* energetically true for you, you conclude its validity, and are ready to act. *An objective experience is indirect, while a subjective experience is direct.* Truth is seen and realized directly, while belief is experienced indirectly. Beliefs are *objects* that the mind creates and clings to. Then mind projects belief "out there" as Truth.

But Truth is never an object "out there" that can be held onto or known.

Truth is the Subject, that which is doing the seeing. But when we objectify Truth, we make it into an object, and we see what we believe and believe what we see. It's a closed loop that we must experience, much like a virtual experience. Since it's happening, we believe it's real, but since it doesn't exist apart from the mind, it is illusory through and through.

The truth is, belief is forever married to doubt. Belief and doubt reside on the same restless coin. If you believe something, it means you really don't know – and there is nothing wrong with that. The problem arises when we think our belief establishes truth. And problems arise when we resist the unknown – which is what we are.

In order to suppress doubt and confusion, the more we believe. The more we firmly believe, the more entrenched and deluded we are.

Despite what we may think – or what we've been taught, belief can never establish truth. No amount of convincing ourselves will ever change this fact. Even firm convictions held in the mind for years can't ever establish truth.

Beliefs are mental constructs created in the mind in order to feel in control of our world. Beliefs are spontaneously created in the mind – and then we take ownership of them, claiming they are "our" beliefs. However, they get created all on their own, without us.

The majority of us approach the big questions in life by constructing a set of ideas and beliefs in our minds – or taking on what others "of authority" tell us about those bigger issues.

We end up depending on them to tell us how life really is, instead of relying on our actual and lived experience to tell us what's really so. Beliefs ultimately fail to provide us the security we seek, because they *can't ever* provide the security we seek.

If we look to belief to provide us lasting security, we're looking in the wrong direction. Generally, beliefs don't lead to the real wisdom that transforms a life. How can something unquestioned and accepted on faith, in the absence of positive knowledge and proof, accomplish this?

We can take solace in the belief that faith is the 'substance of things hoped for, the evidence of things unseen,' but this discovery isn't about hope and faith, not even a little bit.

Faith is merely belief – and in its best form, it becomes trust. You can spin it anyway you want with clever words and supreme logic and reason, but in the end, you just don't know.

This is about non-conceptual realization, that which is beyond belief, faith and hope. Belief, faith and hope are rooted in concepts held in the mind – and the mind can't ever know truth.

If we can't look to our beliefs to make sense of our world and comfort us long term, where do we turn to provide that comfort and security? Instead of depending on our mental constructs (that have no substance or reality because they're literally made up and sustained by our minds) we can look in a different direction.

This "direction" is our actual experience in the moment, prior to belief, and prior to concepts. And that is to just *see* what's actually happening without labeling or describing it. If we want to know what is real, we must confirm in our own experience what's true, without relying on *any* outside source.

Before we label something as "good" or "bad" or "right" or "wrong," we can just be with what is, with equanimity and neutrality – without any preference or bias. Only when we are willing to drop all of our notions, assumptions and opinions about what we think we know in any moment, do we give ourselves the opportunity to really *see what's actual versus what's illusory.*

That fact of being is always present. It is the ground of doubt, and is the doubt-free reality. You know that you are. The awareness of doubt isn't in doubt at all. *Seeing* this, you effortlessly exit from any possible doubts that are raised by the mind – because you *discerned the false from the true.*

The mind may continue to have its doubts, but your being is present, beyond any and all doubt. Do you need a belief to *be* what you are?

See that the mind avoids the unknown like the plague. Notice that the mind feels more safe and secure when it believes in something, even if it hurts. The fact it hurts is a sure sign it's not true.

The mind needs to believe; otherwise, it feels threatened by the unknown. The irony is that which contains and produced the mind *is* unknown. The mind, being a creation, feels threatened by that which created it. You would think the mind would be grateful and bow down to its source – but since the mind can't ever understand its source, it continues in its attempt to be the Final Witness.

It would rather latch onto an illusory concept than nothing at all. It needs content to chew on. Beliefs and concepts are food for the mind. Without them, the mind would starve. It needs to know things, even at the expense of delusion. Many beliefs are functional and good for our physical survival, but fail miserably when it comes to realizing Oneness is the Reality.

In the midst of existential discomfort and pervasive doubt, people make statements like, "You just have to believe," "It's all God's will," "It's not up to me because God is in control" – and in their fear of losing control, they immediately go right back to trying to manipulate the outcome to their liking, further cementing the notion that they are separate and in control.

Emerson said, *"There are many pillows of illusion as flakes in a snowstorm. We wake from one dream into another dream."*

The individual, believing they are a separate entity living in the world, naturally feels out of control and thereby attempts to do something about it. It tries to become something it isn't in order to regain a semblance of control. It's all imagined, even though it feels very real to the dreamer. And yet, it's all perfectly embraced by The Beloved. Being has nowhere to go and no purpose to fulfill, perhaps other than awakening to itself.

In other words, there is no such thing as 'getting it wrong" and there is no such thing as a 'mistake." If what arises can't be any other way, how can it be 'wrong' or a 'mistake?'

If everything you presently "know" and believe in your mind still hasn't revealed what you're looking for, then doesn't it follow that the unknown is where your "answer" lies? Only when you stop insisting that your beliefs establish what's true will you have the opportunity to realize what's true – about yourself and everything else.

But you must be willing to admit that you don't know anything at all. You must be willing to give up all beliefs if you really desire to realize what you Really are. You can maintain the, "If I jump in front of this oncoming train, I'll be splattered all over" survival beliefs. They are good for you and obviously serve a vital function.

This desire to know what you are must be greater than your fear of giving up your lifetime investment in your beliefs about who you are and who your God is. This is critical.

All you suffer from is inattention and your belief system. If you don't have the drive to really discover who you Are, then you will not get past this illusion of your own making that is so adept in the art of deception. There isn't a 'you' to get past an illusion, clearly.

When you *realize* what you are, you realize what everything is, including what "God" is. But you must go beyond belief. Belief is like the stop before the final stop of realization. Seeing that beliefs get created without your intent or decision, you *see* that you are not the author of beliefs – and you never were.

The value of any realization, insight or understanding is only ever in this fresh and new moment. Yesterday's realization isn't fresh. Yesterday is past and we're back in memory again, raising the dead. Clinging to old insights and beliefs is like dancing with the dead. Life is only ever now.

As Zen Master Bankei said, *"Everything is perfectly resolved in the unborn."*

At some point, usually when we've reached the end of our emotional rope – or perhaps when we're ripe enough, we have the opportunity to reorient our priorities away from achievements we think we need to attain in order to be happy and content – to finding out who is chasing the achievements in the first place.

Only when we pause long enough can we see we're like a dog chasing its tail, never seeing we're already in possession of what we're chasing. Only an earnest examination into the very nature of our essence will do. This is all about the essence beneath and behind the appearance – and not the appearance, right?

What you are must be the unseen essence and not any seen appearance.

If a belief gets created spontaneously, without my intent, I can see through it – and discard it. But first, in order to see through it, I need to notice what my experience is as a result of that belief. I can peacefully rest in not knowing – and in that allowance of not knowing (and only until then), the known can reveal itself.

When you clearly see things around you as they are in relation with the whole of your being, there is a maturing, a ripening. You see the false as false, without wasting time and energy figuring out why it is false. Why questions are unimportant and for the mind that seeks control. What happens is simply what happens.

Discarding the false, you're no longer owned by it; it no longer belongs to you. You are out of it and you feel yourself in an atmosphere of perfect clarity – and nothing can pull the rug out from under you.

True realization is only in this present moment, outside of time and beyond belief.

And then a funny thing can happen. You realize what you've been all along – and belief drops away. You laugh at what you conceptually believed yourself to be, and it is seen it could never be conceptualized or believed in.

All the weight from that heavy burden that had been carried for so long is suddenly lifted – and you feel Light.

And you are free, free from all those false concepts once believed in. And it is all because belief was seen for what it is, an illusory notion gone unquestioned, an illusory idea believed in.

See that belief doesn't get you Here.

Chapter 6
Look Until It Is Seen

"God has focused the senses to the outside, therefore man looks outside, not inside. Now and then an adventurous soul, in search of immortality, has looked back and found himself."

– Katha Upanishad

Being on the lazy side, I was happy to find out that realizing what you are is an endeavor that takes little effort. In fact, you don't even have to move a muscle.

You don't need to be in a lotus position, either – and despite the widespread belief in spiritual circles telling you meditation, breathing exercises or purification is essential, you don't have to meditate, breathe a certain way or purify yourself in order to discover your Original Face.

What purification is needed for that which is already eternally pure?

This endeavor is about noticing what is already present. It is not a 'doing,' as that would require effort.

It is before effort, since effort is being witnessed in it. There is no seeking in this endeavor, as the seeking is also witnessed. This witnessing is what you are, and it is prior to, and independent of all that is being witnessed. Simultaneously, it isn't separate from that which appears.

If you say you are the silent witness, what notices that silent witness? Can you find the subject that is aware of the silent witness? Can you say anything about it? Anything you can say about it must mean it is an object in awareness and isn't the Ultimate Reality. Therefore, the silent witness is an object to You.

What you are can't be found.

What you are is even prior to the silent witness.

If you are moved to get into a lotus position and meditate, then by all means, do so. It can definitely be useful, but it is not necessary. The silence sought in meditation is right here, right now. It need not be artificially created. We're all wired differently and meditation just may be the thing that works for you.

The usefulness of sitting in silence lies in the opportunity to still thinking, and to recognize your true nature, that which is prior to thinking. It's an opportunity to see what thinking arises in. And yet, You have this opportunity in each moment, regardless of meditation, regardless of how much noise is present, and regardless of the conditions present.

Reciting mantras and singing chants isn't required, either. However, if you are drawn to do so, have at it. There is no specific 'do this, don't do that' formula for recognizing your Original Face – the face before you were born.

If you look for the one who is supposedly "having" a present experience, the one who is assumed to be "doing" the thinking, seeing and hearing – can you actually find anyone at the center?

Can you even pinpoint a center?

Simply look with naked awareness and see if you can find any solid entity you can call "you" separate from anything else. Look for the person you think you are; can you find it?

Where is this entity you call the "me" located? Where is this reference point you claim is present – you know, the reference point that everything impacts and is referred back to? Where is it centered? If your name is 'Dan' or 'Kim,' where is Dan or Kim centrally located?

Without objectifying anything, what is seen?

Whatever you say is only a concept, a belief. Whatever you say you are isn't what you are. It can't be. Prior to belief or concept, simply look for where you are.

So, where are you?

While there may very well be an idea that there is a "me" within "my body" looking out at "the world" and directing this body/mind through life, owning my thoughts, making my decisions, choosing my actions, behaviors and feelings, is there any evidence of this to be found?

This "me" living inside a body, this "me" that is a separate unit of consciousness possessed with a soul, *is* the Immaculate Misconception.

Is there any spot in the body where you can say, "This is what I am; this is where I start?" Is there any clear distinction between you and not you? Aside from a mental image, a thought, a story about who you *think* you are, can it be seen that there isn't any separate entity encapsulated within a body?

The fact is, you can only *believe or assume* you are a separate entity existing *in* this world. You can't know it. Conversely, you *can* know you aren't a separate entity – and that the world is *within* what you are, but you can only believe you are an individual living in this world.

You can know, without any shred of doubt (because doubt won't arise again) that absolutely nothing is external or separate from what you are. When belief drops away and realization happens, doubt, being the opposing side of belief, drops away.

With rigorous honesty, can you recognize what is effortlessly and always present, before thought-form? It's invisible and form-less, and always present.

Who you believe you are is nothing more than a mental image – and images aren't real.

We'll go deeper into this investigation of what you are in the 'Present Before Thought' and 'The Center-less Center' chapters coming up later, but stay with this investigation right now.

Don't do what most will do and dismiss this. This is the key that opens the vault full of treasures beyond your wildest dreams. This is for Real.

It's really a game of recognition and subtraction, without any expectation of finding anything at all. Recognizing what's already the case is how this game (just a metaphor) is played. When we truly see, we realize what's been true all along.

The fact is, seeing *This* takes no real intelligence. In fact, the intellect and past 'knowledge' is often an obstacle to seeing what you are, simply because it cannot be seen with the intellect. Before thought, belief, faith, opinion and perception, there is only Reality.

Before thinking, Reality just is – whole, perfect and complete, appearing as divided, imperfect and incomplete.

Before you rely on any outside source to tell you what you are, it is instantly and immediately available at anytime. Even right NOW. Nobody can "tell you" what you are. You can only realize and *be* what you are. You can't read in a book what you are, no matter how sacred or regarded that book is.

If you say, "Well, that book, David, happens to be inspired by the word of God." I might say, "If God is all there is, without opposition, tell me what book ever written that wasn't inspired by the word of God?" God is writing the book, through man, as man.

As it says in the Ribhu Gita: *"Abide as That in which there are no holy scriptures or sacred books, no one who thinks, no objection or answer to it, no theory to be rejected, nothing other than the one Self – and be always happy, free from the least trace of thought."*

Why rely on anything other than your own ability to see? You have to take a look and see for yourself what is true in your own experience instead of relying on beliefs, dogma, faith and tradition. It is worth reiterating: the desire to see what's real must be greater than your fear of what may happen to your investment in your beliefs.

God or Reality cannot be approached by belief or anything you ever read, or will read. You can read something and conclude, "Yes, that's it — that's the truth, and it even feels true."

But can you absolutely confirm it is true, without a shred of doubt? No, you can't.

And it's not a looking "out there" at objects in our awareness. What we are isn't an object. What we are is the Subject. It's a 180-degree turn of attention inward, to look and see what's doing the looking.

In Christianity, *repent* didn't mean to atone for your sins, but to "turn your attention inward and see everything anew" — and notice what is doing the looking.

As Anthony de Mello once said, *"When you repent for your past, realize it's a great religious distraction to waking up. Wake up! Stop all the crying. Understand. Wake up!"*

The original meaning of sin is "missing the mark," not some thought or behavior God looks down upon.

When seeking happens, a looking "out" for an object naturally occurs. You are the Subject in which all objects appear. This is why you hear, "Seek and you won't find." You won't find what you are because in order to find anything, you need an object to be found.

You are that which you seek, long before you seek.

Relaxing back into this presence that contains everything, allowing everything to come and go as it does, how is your experience different? What is felt?

Our minds are wired to look out at sensations, ideas, similarities and differences — and anything noisy that clamors for our attention. Rather than falling into the habitual patterns of looking 'out there,' take the backward step, as they say in Zen.

This is a very simple thing, but the mind often usurps the moment and insists it "should" be more difficult than it is. And when identification happens with mind, we hop on the train of thought and go for a ride, often a very long ride. And what happens when an argument with reality occurs? Contraction becomes the experience, does it not?

In our argument with what is, we sever the possibility of any peace and freedom whatsoever. And yet, that peace and freedom never left us.

Witness what comes and goes – and find out what remains. Reality doesn't come and go. Indian Sage Ramana Maharshi said, *"Let what comes come, let what goes, go. Find out what remains."*

Is there ever a time you are not? If not, you must be the Reality you seek.

This is the Kingdom of Heaven Jesus often spoke of. Jesus pointed to the only reality, this present moment, and referred to it as the "Kingdom of Heaven." He didn't mean it was some place where "good" souls go after physical death.

Looking for yourself doesn't mean leaning on any outside source, including teachers, gurus, bibles, scriptures, sutras and the like. You are the final authority and self-realization only happens within, in your own experience. No one can give you what you already are. No one can tell you what you are.

If the message here is: "You are already that which you seek," then look and see if this is the case. This is all about remembering, not learning.

Learning implies you don't already know.

If you really are the Formless, Empty, Knowing Presence of Awareness that everything arises from and falls back into, you must investigate in your own experience to see if this is true.

This is an inside game – and you can never rely on another to tell you what you are.

If you've been told you are this Clear, Empty, Awake and Aware Space that is eternally untouched by anything, look and see for yourself whether this is true or not. Believing in it matters not.

Until you *know* first-hand, without any doubt whatsoever, you're just messing around with stale concepts that have no aliveness in them. You're just hanging out at the surface, treading water.

Dive deep.

It's right Here.

You are the aliveness and boundlessness you seek – and until you discover this for yourself, what good is any of this to you? Why would you ever accept the word of anyone else, no matter how highly regarded they are, no matter how beautiful and flowery the words are?

Jesus or the Buddha himself could show up at your doorstep and eloquently tell you wonderful things about what you are – things you've never heard – but unless YOU know, of what value are their words? Believing words only provides a false sense of security.

Believing only provides a false sense of identity. Don't take up *anything* as true until you confirm it for yourself.

What you really are is the complete absence of fear. Notice the fear present in the questioning of what you believe is true. It's not only natural, but it is understandable, isn't it? Let it be there.

What you really are is the unconditional love and compassion that welcomes all fear. Just look.

Anything less than pure and direct knowing of what you are, beyond any doubt, is simply hearsay. How will you know when you know, you might ask? The question and the questioner fall away. All doubt will leave your system, never to come back.

Life is the answer – and there's never a doubt about it.

And you'll know it in every fiber of your being. There is no more resistance to life. If there is, even that is welcomed in what you are. No matter what, all is well, especially when it appears not to be.

That's how you know.

We can hear the words of Buddha when he said, *"When you realize how perfect everything is, you will tilt your head back and laugh at the sky."*

43

See through your belief that you don't have the means necessary to awaken to what you are.

You do.

However, the desire must be real. You can't fool the universe.

Chapter 7
What Is Real

"Nothing real can be threatened. Nothing unreal exists. Herein lies the peace of God."

– A Course in Miracles

What is real – and what is imagined?

When I don't know what is real, I remain in an illusory world of my own making. And when I cannot discern the real from the false, it hurts. Steeped in illusion that fractures, I can only feel divided inside.

Wholeness, being ever-present, is something longed for. What is ever-present is what is real.

The amount of suffering the body/mind experiences is always relative to its ability to discern truth from fiction.

The real does not die; the unreal never lived. The unreal is illusory and can only appear for a bit, and then disappear back into the nothingness from which it came.

Reality never changes.

What is it that you *really* want? Do you know?

If what is imagined can be seen, can it ever be real? Can what is real be seen?

Only the unseen is real. The seen is never the real.

You are the Unseen Seer and not anything that can be seen.

Image-nation consists of changing images and concepts that temporarily appear in awareness. Therefore, neither is real.

Anticipating an undesired future moment is anticipation and imagination. Imagining there *is* a future moment is the perception of time. Therefore, imagination needs time.

Time is a mental construct. Time is mind.

If imagination gives you difficulty, it simply means you take the images and thoughts the mind creates to be real, either running away from them anticipating pain, or clinging to them, desiring pleasure to last.

What is real can never be imagined; what is imagined is never real.

Since belief can never capture Truth or Reality – and can never establish what is true, it is unreal. Why do you think so many suffer from their beliefs? The reason is simple. Because beliefs change, they can't be real. What changes is illusory – and illusion hurts.

If beliefs can be seen and known, can they be real? Only the unseen is real.

Belief in the unreal divides and fractures, and there is no escaping that experience. What is real never divides, never hurts.

What is the common denominator in all your problems? Isn't it the "you", the "me", the "I" you call yourself? If the "I" thought is seen to be unreal and the *cause* of all your troubles, what must happen to the effects?

When the "I" and the "me" thought are *seen* to be imagination, what YOU REALLY ARE reveals itself as that which never left in the first place.

Allow your fiction to come to an end, because on the other side of your fiction is Reality, beautiful and true. In the midst of your fiction,

Reality is. It's not really even accurate to say, "Allow your fiction to end." Who is present to even have a fiction?

Instead, see through the fiction. See there is no one here to *have* a fiction – and watch the fiction end. Within the fiction is Reality, waiting to be discovered. There is nothing to 'get rid of.'

You need only see.

Fictions are created when there is a taking ownership of the stories the mind constructs. Discover the dimension in you prior to stories – that dimension without any concept of story, strife and struggle. This is the dimension you are, the quality-less foundation where all qualities arise.

Wipe the slate clean, empty your cup and come with open arms. You are this clean slate already, untouched and unharmed by all of it. Simply and effortlessly notice that which already welcomes all as it is.

The ego personality has the habit of claiming to be the primary seer, rejecting this and wanting that. However, being witnessed and known by YOU, the Subject, the ego personality is part of the passing scenery.

If it's part of the passing scene, then it must be an object in Consciousness. Consequently, the personality, the imagined self, can never be the final Witness, just as a wave cannot see the ocean.

Awareness is not a thought or feeling. Thoughts and feelings arise in awareness. Awareness is always present, never coming or going. It is forever unharmed by thought and feeling – and is the Real.

Awareness is not a sensation. All sensations arise in the presence of awareness.

Pain and pleasure happen in the timeless now and aren't a problem to awareness, what you really are. The body is a never-ending flow of sensations. Thinking is a never-ending flow of thoughts and images.

What is seeing these sensations, thoughts and images? Wouldn't YOU have to be prior in order to witness them?

Is the awareness of pain in pain? Is the awareness of pleasure in pleasure?

Images, beliefs, sensations and experience are all passing phenomena with no independent existence apart from awareness of it coming and going. They are in a constant parade, marching in front of that which never changes, that which sees it.

They are all relative to the Real – and have no absolute Reality. Confuse what you are with this constant parade, and you cannot escape the effects of that perception. Confuse what you are with the passing show that happens by itself, and you remain in bondage.

Even Houdini couldn't escape this. This fusion is the straitjacket of all straitjackets.

Freedom is in the realization of the wisdom of no escape; it's in the recognition that there isn't anyone present to escape anything. This isn't about belief; this is nothing short of a radical shift in perception, beyond belief or anything the mind can conceive.

When what is true is truly seen, this shift in perception happens on its own.

This is the restoration of true perception – seeing as Life sees – seeing as God sees. In Sufism it is said, *"The eye with which I see God with is the same eye with which God sees me."* *"It is in this realization that the soul enters the kingdom of God."*

It is one seeing, one knowing and one love.

Bob Marley had it right!

Without you, content-free Awareness, nothing is. Without you, content-free Awareness, pleasure and pain can't even be experienced. Pain and pleasure have no independent existence and therefore, is unreal. Emotions are objects seen, felt and known, and merely phenomena passing through – and unreal.

This isn't to imply ignoring them; it simply means they come and go. As they come up, allow them to be. They appear, stay for a bit, and then pass on.

Emotions still arise in the body/mind, but when there is no one there to take delivery of them, there's no great charge anymore. Put simply, there's just an emotion that arises, living for a few moments and is no more.

Nothing can live long in This.

Pain and pleasure are objects felt in the body, within pure, content-free awareness. The objects of pleasure are remembered and desired again; the objects of pain are remembered and avoided.

Suffering never happens in presence. Suffering needs time, and time is mind. Even though suffering *feels* real to the dreamer, it isn't real. All feelings and sensations are transient and therefore, unreal.

What is real must be eternally present.

What is unreal comes and goes, is seen and known.

Desire is the memory of pleasure and the imagined pleasure derived from a future event.

Fear is the memory of pain and the imagination of a future undesired event.

For suffering to arise, the belief in the "me" must be present. In the absence of the "me," there isn't anyone taking ownership of any aspect of experience, including fear and desire.

In fact, there are no problems in presence. There are no problems unless you think about them, are there? Thinking must be present in order for suffering to happen.

But what are you?

Timeless Being, here and now, is always problem free. Timeless being, the Real, is that which contains the mind that creates the problem. Minds create problems only to look for solutions for them. It's an endless loop, until it is seen for what it is, an object in the awareness you are.

Mind isn't separate from what you are. Nothing is.

All exists now. All there is – is now. There isn't a past, present and future. Thinking divides the One into the Many, and believes the now is the moment that exists between a past and future.

There is only ever now. Everything else is but a dream imagined, literally. Imagination is not reality, but happens in reality. Nothing is to be rejected or accepted. Just see what is real. That is all.

See all that is false and find out what remains. What remains is the Real.

Absolutely everything is appearance only, on the Screen of Awareness you are. Being the Screen itself, YOU are untouched, unharmed.

The unreal appears within the Real – and is none other than the Real. Identify with the unreal and suffer.

The "I" thought is the birth of fear – and fear brings about insecurity and vulnerability. Insecurity and vulnerability are the driving force behind becoming.

Fear is born of separation, which isn't real, only imagined. Imagination imagines separation. It is an unreal thought imagining another unreal thought – within what you are, the REAL.

There is nothing wrong with desire. Humans desire. It comes with the package. Attachment to desire is the cause of suffering. There isn't anything wrong with desire, but see every "thing" you desire is imaginary. Every "thing" you fear is imaginary.

The "you" that desires and fears is imaginary and unreal. Before the "I" thought, Reality is – untouched by desire and fear.

The truest freedom is not wanting.

See that what you *really* want is what you are – the Ultimate Reality. All desires are nothing other than a longing to be whole and complete.

All desires are a longing to come home – and to simply rest in Being.

Your deepest longings have already been fulfilled, but it has gone unrealized. Absolutely everything you have ever desired is already present, right now.

And the last place you would ever look is right here, right now.

What is real is right here, right now.

Chapter 8
The Granddaddy Illusion

"The light of the body is the eye: Therefore, when thine eye is single, your whole body will be filled with light."

– Luke (11:14)

Separation is the primary illusion that all other illusions are derived.

We seek because we feel separate – and we feel separate when we seek. We feel separate from each other and from life, but are we really separate? What speaks of this separation? Can we find it in nature?

Are boundaries actually real – or are they simply imagined products of the mind that are designed to divide and separate?

What does this sense of separateness appear to? To whom does it appear in? Could it be possible that the resolution of your sense of separateness is perfectly resolved in the Inseparable One that eternally embraces your sense of separateness?

All there is, is Wholeness – the One, Infinite Energy appearing as everything... the oceans, the sky, human beings, cars, horns honking, grass growing, trees blooming, leaves falling, birds chirping, bees stinging, babies crying, lovers arguing and enemies killing – and *whatever* else you can come up with.

It is the Inexpressible No-thing appearing as absolutely Every-thing.

In other words, all there is – is No-thing Being Everything. No exceptions. Not a one. Everything arises out of nothing, appearing as everything. Each arising is totally fresh and new, just like this sentence.

There is nothing that is apart – or divided from the Unbounded Everything – and yet, *because* it is free (and devoid) of any and all characteristics, experience, attribute, and time, it can appear separate from itself, seemingly in time.

Because it's empty of all that, it can contain all that – all the characteristics, experience, attribute and time.

The Unchanging, Content-free Space contains all changing content.

All content arises liberated. In other words, all things appear dualistically with an opposite, and what appears is already free. Love arises in unison with fear, always. Peace arises in unison with conflict, always. In order to experience peace, one must be able to experience conflict.

In order to experience love, fear and hate must be a potential experience.

Letting it be as it is, fear and conflict transforms into love and peace, rather quickly. Fear is not separate from love. Conflict is not separate from peace. They are one appearing as two.

What is paid attention to is what will manifest. Resisting the fear, you give life to what you don't want and love seems distant. Resisting the conflict, you give life to what you don't want and peace eludes you.

Everything is simply a manifestation of One, Eternal Movie playing out – and despite the appearance of so many different characters, the essence behind those actors isn't separate at all.

It is the One You Are.

What's peering through all the actors on the stage of life is the One appearing as the Many. The actors appear different, but they aren't separate from the singular essence that unites them.

Since intelligence-energy is eternally boundless and free, it has the ability to contract and restrict itself in a human being, all the while being whole, unbounded and complete.

What apparently arises from that is a sense of separation, out of which springs a particular sense of identity – a unique self-consciousness that believes it is separate from everything else.

This is reality for most people.

Incidentally, this is also the birth of suffering. This is where it all started, in The Garden of Eden, if you will. When man ate the forbidden fruit from the tree of knowledge of good and evil, he was expelled from the Garden and the seeming divide was created.

The Garden is the place of unity, of non-duality of good and evil, male and female, right and wrong, and God and human beings.

Eating from duality, you are cast out. No longer seeing the unity behind apparent division, human suffering was born.

The energetic component of seeking pleasure and avoiding pain began here as well.

The "me" is born and the "I" thought becomes the reference point that all experience gets referred back to. And "my" story begins, as well as "my" suffering. The belief becomes, "I am my story – and without 'me,' there is no story."

Absolutely everything seems to be personally experienced as a series of happenings, subject to real time, happening to a real me.

It *feels* incredibly real to the dreamer. And what *feels* real is sustained, believed, acted on and reinforced – and we remain on the wheel of suffering.

Since the mind can only think dualistically, it divides everything up into a subject/object split. Everything becomes about "me" experiencing this that I like and this that I don't like. And the quality of my experience is determined mostly by experiencing what I want through effort and achievement – and avoiding what I don't want with resistance and denial.

Within the story, ideas like choice, free will, purpose, enlightenment, spirituality and journeys in time are played out and also seem to be real. Not only is this sense of separation just a thought, inherent in that thought is a contraction of energy throughout the entire body/mind impacting every experience.

Separation and contraction go hand in hand.

Within this belief in separation comes the idea of becoming. We've been taught since childhood in order to have a happy and successful life, we have to become "somebody" in this world. We're told if we want the respect of others, we need to 'be somebody' who earns respect.

Rarely is it ever pointed out to us that we already are what we seek, and that absolutely nothing is needed. Rarely is it pointed out to us that we are the One Reality, as we are – appearing as a separate individual, within a dream of separation.

As long as there is a belief in separation, there will always be a sense of lack and inadequacy. With that sense of lack, a desire for resolution arises and we strive to become something "more" or "better" than we are, further solidifying the sense of being someone separate who is lacking.

It is Being dreaming it is other than itself, pretending to be divided against itself, looking everywhere for that which It thinks It has lost – and that which It thinks It doesn't have. All the while it IS Everything. All the while, nothing was ever lost, nothing ever needed, and nothing ever to be gained.

Being *is* Dorothy dreaming she isn't already Home.

Illusion is a very powerful force – and in a hypnotic, trance-like dream of separation, it feels very real for the dreamer. Closed off to the possibility that just maybe what the dreamer is really looking for is beyond belief and imagination, the dream continues.

On occasion, when reality is seen as it is, without any self-reference or judgment, expansion and peace arises. Conversely, when the "me" searches for peace and freedom, it is not seen.

The searching suppresses the peace that is longed for.

And yet, the "me" isn't what will experience the peace and freedom it longs for. Egos don't get to experience peace and freedom. True and total freedom has nothing to do with getting rid of our human weaknesses and perceived imperfections. Rather, it is the full embrace of them, as they are.

And yet, "we" don't have to try to embrace anything. When it is recognized that everything is already deeply accepted as it arises, no effort is necessary because it's already a done deal.

True freedom has nothing to do with the "me" we have identified with, but has everything to do with that which the "me" appears in.

In seeing, an open expanse and spaciousness is felt because, for whatever reason, the mind wasn't usurping the moment. The veil of separation is temporarily lifted and all discontent and identification with the story of "me" disappears.

And then the mind tries to cling to *that* experience to make it last.

And when the mind clings to make it last, the experience ceases.

In that timeless moment, self-consciousness steps in and says, "I don't want this feeling of peace and freedom to end – and I wish it could be this way all the time." Pop. Experience over. The mind divides the experience up between subject (me) and object (not me), labeling it as either good or bad, desired or undesired – and back comes the "me" to the center.

Division can only bring pain. Union brings peace.

In order to 'get away from it all,' many watch endless movies and/ or television, constantly read books or surf the Internet in order to be distracted or "entertained." We tell ourselves we need a break from all of it, when we really need a break from the "me."

It's like *we're* sending *ourselves* on a short vacation, so WE can relax and have a good time.

We just want to disappear for a while. Funny thing is, the "me" that wants to disappear doesn't even exist.

We run from the sense of separation because it hurts – all the while looking for the wholeness we already are.

With a sense of separation comes a certain degree of dissatisfaction – a sense that something is missing. We can't ever put our finger on what is missing, but we just know something isn't right or we wouldn't be feeling dissatisfied, longing for something different than what we have.

Only when there is an opening to the possibility of that which is beyond self-centered thinking, can the contracted energy dissolve back into the unbounded freedom it already is. Until then, it's simply boundless energy allowing itself to be bound, all within the appearance of a particular body/mind, within the freedom you already are.

Only when there is an opening to the possibility that perhaps maybe the sense of separation has been the cause of all our problems, can there be a seeing that it was a fiction all along.

The idea of someone who needs to be liberated from something drops away in the simple seeing there never was anyone who needed anything. The dream of separation ends upon the full recognition that All is One. Struggle and effort drop away quite naturally.

Who is present to struggle and effort for that which never left in the first place?

Timeless Being requires no path to it. It's Here, now. Presence of Being demands nothing.

It is the Gentle Constant where all demands and requirements arise in. It sits back and enjoys its own show. It is the writer, producer, actors, the stage and the screen upon which it plays.

It sits back in wonder and curiosity, celebrating its own Play.

There is no love separate from the one who longs for it. There aren't any lovers anywhere to be found. There is only love, in love with itself – and cannot be fractured, divided or torn apart.

It is beyond any harm.

It is so simple it confounds the mind.

Chapter 9
A Timeless Now

"Past and future are simply aspects of the Infinite Presence extending beyond the limited recognition of the conscious mind – which extrapolates based on the finite and the familiar. Learn to recognize this habit of mind, and trust Awareness as it arises – always inherent here and now."

– Metta Zetty

Reality is always right now. The only reality is this timeless moment. Everything else is but a dream.

The mind lives in time, YOU don't. Minds can't see this, but YOU can. If you are identified with the mind, you believe in the existence of time.

Looking intently, can you find any evidence whatsoever of time in this present moment?

I used to think eternity meant forever and ever, in time. Eternity means outside the stream of time. It doesn't mean everlasting time, but a moment *without* time.

The belief in time, along with the belief in separation and individuality can be said to be the cause of all your troubles. To awaken to what you are is to literally awaken *from* time – and to *see* there is only ever a timeless now.

Being timeless, all of Eternity is wholly and completely present at every point in time. To the Eye of Eternity, all of it is always and already present right now, in this timeless moment. Thus, the *entire* Absolute, The All That Is, is completely present at every point of space and time.

Now implies a moment between a past and a future, but now isn't sandwiched between the last moment and the next moment. There is no past or future. Past is memory only and future is anticipation or imagination.

Both are mental concepts believed to be real.

Granted, it appears that there is a past and future, but Reality is beyond time and appearances – and always now.

In Truth, there really isn't a now. Now is a concept. There is just This, that which presents itself, timelessly.

While everything appears and disappears in presence, including thoughts, feelings, sensations and experiences, to the mind it seems that time is lapsing. Cars, houses, bodies, skin, flowers, animals and everything in the manifest world decays and one day, dies.

Ramesh Balsekar said, *"It is not the present which is fleeting past us with sickening speed. The present moment is indeed eternal. It is our imperfect perception that creates the horizontal succession in time. Sequential duration is a consequence of a single-track verbalization of our split-mind, which does not grasp the outer world instantaneously but interprets in perversely by extracting bits and pieces and calling them things and events."*

Quantum physicists and Neuro-scientists have finally caught up with what the Seers and Sages have been saying for ages: There is no time; everything constantly changes, and absolutely nothing has any solidity at all.

Matter and time are both illusory.

Although humans cannot perceive it, everything is constantly flashing in and out of existence (including sensation and thinking) each nanosecond. Everything is vibrating energy, flashing in and out of the timeless now. Everything we can see and observe in the manifest world lives in time and has a particular shelf life.

What is born is subject to time and therefore, must perish.

So, everything is popping in and out of existence, except what I am. While the mind is incredibly complex, amazing and very useful for many things, it can't see this. Describing or labeling what flashes in and out is always delayed. As fast as the mind is, it can't keep up. Even if it wasn't delayed, the description can never be the described.

Once it pops in, poof, it completely disappears and no longer exists. Mind either latches onto it or avoids it, giving life to a dead thing. Both movements create the illusion of time.

"Let the dead bury the dead."

We bring a dead thing to life through our resistance, judgment, and wishing it was different than it is. This is the energy that feeds and gives life to the dead, resurrecting what already disappeared. Resurrecting the dead never feels quite right – because it's illusory. All the while, we continue to reinforce the sense of "me" that is experiencing all that.

Lazarus would surely be impressed with all the things we bring back to life!

All thought is past. As soon as it arises, it is gone. As soon as thought arises, the next sensation or thought arises, no longer to exist. All sensations are past. YOU are now. YOU *are* this moment – the timeless being in which all temporal thoughts and sensations emerge.

Never being able to know anything in This timeless, fresh and new moment, there is a constant recognition of what I really am, even in the midst of a painful situation. If this moment is always fresh and new, how can anything be known other than what I am?

Without referencing thought or the past, without referencing your favorite quotes or clichés – and without memory or opinion, in this moment, right where you are, what do you know for sure? Other than the fact of being – other than the fact you are – is there anything you can know in this moment?

If you really look deeply, it is seen you can't know anything in this moment but what you are. In this recognition, all questions and answers dissolve because Life is the answer.

Thoughts about the past and thoughts about the future are always present thoughts. Memory is always a *present* experience. Whenever something is remembered, it is remembered presently.

Even the most seemingly real memories of the past and the most vividly imagined scenarios of the future both occur in this vast, open, content-free timeless now. Nothing ever happens outside of now.

Other than the fact of your own being, nothing can be known in this unknown, timeless now.

To be clear, there is no "you" *and* this moment. There is no such thing as "be here now." This is a dualistic statement, for there is no "you" that *can* be here now.

There is only now – and what you are *is* the timeless now, in its entirety, without separation.

You are the Timeless Now that everything comes and goes in. You are the changeless capacity for all that changes.

Awaken from the concept of time!

Chapter 10
Fear, Guilt & Shame

"In the sky, there is no distinction of east and west; people create distinctions out of their own minds and then believe them to be true."

– Buddha

When I don't know what I really am, fear has a tendency to be the driving force in my life. However subtle, it lurks in the background, like a tiger, ready to pounce when my sense of identity is challenged.

What I fear most is the absence of myself; what I desire most is the absence of myself.

When I fear the absence of myself, I reinforce the belief in the dream of individuality, which keeps me asleep and prone to further pain and suffering. Fearing pain, I seek to gain pleasure.

When I seek to gain pleasure, I am in fear of future pain. It is an endless loop in time, that is, until I recognize what I really am.

When I fear no longer existing, I cling to security and survival, two concepts that have no reality. Fearing my own demise, I believe in a beginning and an end.

Believing in a beginning and an end, I naturally desire to postpone that end. In seeing what I am, the concepts of a beginning and an end drop away.

Fearing vulnerability, I strive to be strong. Fearing insecurity, I strive to be secure and project what I am not. Fearing intimacy, I strive to be indifferent.

If I fear being nobody, I strive to be somebody. The things I fear seem to be in a constant shuffle, a game of musical chairs in which I am always trying to find a place to sit.

When I view these emotions as a simple 'fact of life," and not something self-generated, once one is overcome, another appears to take its place.

We say, "I am afraid." Are you really the one who is afraid? Is it true that you are the one in fear?

Might it be that you are simply the boundless capacity and space for fear, the vastness in which fear comes and goes?

Dear One, do not be afraid to stop pretending to be what you are not.

We say, "I am in pain." Are you really the one in pain? Is it true that you are the one who suffers – and you are the one who feels shame? Are you the character caught in the story of the "me" who suffers in time – or are you the timeless, spacious freedom for all the pain, shame and suffering to come and go in?

You are never "the fearful one" – and you are never "the one in pain or shame." You are the wide-open capacity that *is* life itself – where guilt, fear and pain are allowed. Even your non-acceptance and judgment of guilt and fear is most welcome in what you are.

If I believe I am a separate person living in this world, fear must arise. Fear is born of separation and my life becomes an ongoing negotiation and management of all that I fear.

Feeling separate, I take things very personally and am inclined to compare, resist, envy and judge "others" according to my belief systems, values and opinions.

Believing that the purpose and meaning of my life is to strive to become more than I already am (and to make my life work) I am often left feeling guilty when I don't live up to the standard I set for myself.

I feel guilty when I "get off track" and therefore, reinsert myself back on the path of improvement in order to reach my goals.

In fact, I can only feel guilty when I haven't lived up to my own expectation I have for myself – or from those that have been imposed upon me.

When I take personal responsibility for the lives of others, especially my adult children, I am left feeling guilty and ashamed.

I am left in fear of what will happen to them 'some' day and see their success or failure as a reflection of the kind of parent I was. I don't see that I could not have been any different a parent than I was – and I suffer. I don't see that they are solely responsible for their own lives. I may say I do, but I don't live what I know.

Instead, I beat myself up with illusory "could haves" and "should haves" – and I usurp that responsibility and take it on. In this way, I confirm that I don't really know that they are solely responsible for their own lives.

When I do know, I am able to be truly compassionate and supportive without any sense of guilt and shame. No longer coming from inner division, I am a place of refuge for those I love most.

This is what it means to be of real service.

Real service and compassion can only come when inner division is completely absent.

When I experience fear, guilt and shame, it means I am identified with this limited body/mind, and not that which is seeing all of it. My fear, guilt and shame thrive on inattention.

They cannot stand being clearly seen. They don't hold up to close examination.

Once thoroughly examined, the fictitious entity dissolves in the Clear Light of Seeing.

In presence, there is no becoming. In presence, there is only now; becoming involves time. In seeing that there is no one living this life and that life is living itself through this body/mind, fear, guilt and shame drop away.

When I know what I am, illusory fear, guilt and shame don't get created anymore. Fear, guilt and shame need time – and I am now, fear-less, guilt-less and shame-less, eternally.

As long as I continue to pay attention and buy into my story of what 'should be' and what 'should have' happened, I remain paralyzed. As long as my energy goes into indulging in my sense of guilt and shame, I continue to sever any possibility of seeing what I am – and I remain in fear.

Liberation becomes a "nice idea" for others, but not for me.

For me, liberation is just a concept.

After all, I am too enmeshed and identified with my fear, guilt and shame to look at what I really am. I am too attached to my suffering that without it, I wouldn't know who I am. I am comfortable in my suffering – at least I know it.

The unknown is scary.

In my shame and self-blame, I cut off any possibility to see it can't be any different than it presently is – and fear drives much of my life. Whenever there is war inside, there is war outside. Creating an identity around 'my struggles,' who would I be *without* all that inner division and pain?

What payoffs would I have to surrender?

There seems to be a real fascination inherent with taking ownership of other people's issues and neurosis. We get to take credit for "caring" at the expense of our own suffering. The drama provides payoffs.

Instead of placing my attention on that which is beyond and untouched by all of it, in a trance-like state, I remain mired in illusory concepts of right and wrong, good and bad, worthy and unworthy.

It is an effective strategy the mind employs to misguide and discourage the clear recognition of its Original Face – what it arises in. Meanwhile, the opportunity to rediscover that face is instantly available.

However, as long as there is a continuance of ceaseless self-judgment and criticism, I remain enslaved in an existence of fear, condemnation, guilt, shame, blame and remorse.

Even fear, guilt, shame and pain want to come to rest. After expressing itself, it simply wants to rest, but we're too caught up in trying to get rid of it, numb out to it, or run away from it.

Any movement is a movement away – and we lock in place what we don't want.

I suffer trying to appease a God of my own making, when I AM that God projected.

When I remain attached to my own suffering, I don't see that Grace, the ever-present force that has the power to release me of my delusion, is right here, right now.

In my refusal to look for myself, and in my refusal to see my way *isn't* working, I cut off the very possibility of that release.

Attempting to console myself, I tell myself I am a 'good, caring person' because a good, caring person wouldn't care so much. After all, a good, caring person wouldn't feel so much.

I get to give myself credit for "stepping up to the plate" and taking on the suffering of those who I care for – and I remain in a bed of my own illusions – and it hurts.

All the while, each feeling, each experience and each illusory concept I entertain is a doorway to the freedom I really desire. If only I could give up the investment in "me," I'd be able to see a way out of the predicament I find myself in.

Attached to and identified with my suffering, I keep the veil of individuality and separation in place.

In taking delivery of all of it, I remain the landing spot for all that

I'd rather not experience. And still, all of it is an invitation to see what I really am.

Not seeing that I keep everything alive with my own guilt, resistance and self-judgment, I strengthen and reinforce what I don't want. In my insistence on taking responsibility for other's pain and trauma, I continue to dance with the dead and keep alive the story that keeps me imprisoned.

Conversely, realizing you can never be the source of my pain, and that I was never the source of *your* pain, I no longer need to fear, punish or avoid you. Seeing that no one has ever harmed me, there isn't anyone to forgive.

Much of Christianity is based upon forgiveness. Ironically, it completely misses the mark (sin), as there is nothing to forgive because no one ever wronged me. If no one ever 'did me wrong,' who or what is there to absolve? What confession is needed? Who would confess to whom?

Granted, egos can be bruised, pride can be questioned, but who I really am has never been stained. In this recognition, I rest in a deep peace, never being a victim of anything, including my own thinking.

Never did I have a single enemy.

If our love is dependent on physical beauty, when beauty fades, our love fades. If our love is dependent on feelings, when feelings fade, our love is compromised. If our love is associated with stories, when stories are forgotten, so is our love.

And if our love latches onto time and form, when form perishes, time-bound love dies, too.

Presence, prior to my story about my life, forever remains right here, right now. It is untouched by the passing show appearing in Consciousness.

If the story that produced the fear and guilt is seen not to have an author, no longer is there "my" fear, "my" guilt, or "my" shame.

It is simply seen for what it is, as it is – simply raw emotion emerging to express itself.

No longer using labels to describe any of it, all that is left are sensations coming and going in the welcoming, changeless presence I am. Seeing what all sensation arises in, no longer is there any resistance to any of it. As a result, they don't stick around long.

Ceasing to own any aspect of experience, there's an intimacy and greater ability to respond in a loving and compassionate way.

If anger and frustration arises, then anger and frustration arises. It's not a problem. Even in pain, there is still peace. The peace underlies all of that phenomenal expression – and it is palpable.

This peace is felt, and not just believed in – no matter what.

This isn't the case for the involved individual. The individual says, "I shouldn't be angry or frustrated; I should deal with this better."

And what we resist persists.

Ceasing to identify with any of it, I am freed from the bondage that once enslaved me, and my presence impacts those around me in a way I only imagined.

Paradoxically, when there is no one who takes delivery of sensation and emotion, there's an intimacy with the ten thousand things that arise.

All expression is allowed in what I am.

Turning my attention from the investment in my old story that brought so much pain and suffering, to the sensations arising in the body, an ease of being arises and I get a taste of freedom.

What I meet head on cannot torture. Seeing that everything happens within awareness, nothing can harm me because nothing is outside or apart from me.

Knowing that words only point, there is a refraining from labeling any sensation. Up comes one sensation for a bit, only to disappear to allow another to arise for a bit.

It's a formless dance, not always in sync, but a dance, nonetheless.

It is a Grand Orchestration of the Highest Order, never needing to be understood, yet always to be celebrated and lived.

All questions and answers dissolve in the recognition that Life has always been the answer.

If I really look and see, I notice I don't have control over any of it. Nevertheless, in the absence of any resistance to what is, it is seen for what it is, an eternal dance to be enjoyed by the One I Am.

And all fear, guilt and shame dissolve back into the nothingness from which it came.

I rest in the peace and freedom that I used to seek.

Chapter 11
Everything Is Appearance Only

"The collective disease of humanity is that people are so engrossed in what happens, so hypnotized by the world of fluctuating forms, so absorbed in the content of their lives, they have forgotten the essence, that which is beyond content, beyond form, beyond thought. They are so consumed by time they have forgotten eternity, which is their origin, home, and destiny. Eternity is the living reality of who you are."
– Eckhart Tolle

Whatever drops away isn't real to begin with.

Everything is simply appearance, except what you really are. Every appearance is temporal. You are not.

If it were not for You, nothing could ever appear. Without the eternal You, the transience of all things couldn't happen. All appearance have no independent nature apart from the empty space of Knowing awareness it appears in.

Looking into all experience and sensation, it is seen that absolutely everything drops away, except what you really are. Don't believe a word you read here. Find out and confirm for yourself whether this is true or not. Relying on anyone else is second-hand and merely hearsay.

The entire visible world, the world of form, is the world of the manifest. It is a world of phenomena – that which appears to be. Absolutely every "thing" is impermanent, with a beginning, middle and end – including the "you" you think you are. All appearances have a certain life span.

After all, what is born must die.

You are the un-manifest, the No-thing that absolutely everything appears in. The opposite of phenomena is noumenon – which means, "that which is." That which is, the un-manifest, is the formless Reality from which every form emerges. Reality, or that which never changes, is what all phenomena comes and goes in.

It is the unchanging, un-manifest Reality You are.

The "you" you think you are, is also appearance only – happening within what you are. You are not the body, that which you drive around in all day – and that which is seen and known. You are not the mind, the activity of thinking that attempts to 'know' everything as it arises.

The ego-personality, the person who believes they are a separate entity is simply changing phenomena appearing in the unchanging, aware, emptiness You are. All that is left is You – the One that is looking through the eyes of the body that you travel around through.

Generally, we say, "Everything I see appears to *me*." We say, "This is *my* appearance and I appear in the world." The "me" *becomes* the reference point – the self-center – that everything appears to.

However, what we're expressing as *is* the passing appearance of that which contains all appearances.

See that the world appears within what you are – and is phenomena, just like everything else. It is very obvious. Just stop conceptualizing and see what is naturally the case. The mind tells you a story of separation and division, but where is this separation and division?

Can it be found?

What are the appearances happening to? What are they happening in? Does fear, doubt and worry happen to you – or does it happen in a fear-less, doubt-less and worry-free awareness? See that thinking, feeling and experience happen in the clear, naked and empty awareness You are, that which is before the mind.

Once you really *see* appearances don't happen to "you," including thoughts, feelings and sensations, and that they happen in the empty, awake, welcoming aware space You are, you won't care what is arising. No longer will you be identified with the body/mind that seeks pleasure and avoids pain...

And off the wheel of suffering you go.

Life still goes on. Life continues to happen. There can be pleasurable days and not so pleasurable days. It doesn't really matter anymore because there isn't any concern about what 'may' happen or what has already happened.

Resting in what is, and resting in the unharmed awareness you are, is there a threat anymore?

Who is threatened?

After all, what are they occurring to? What are they occurring in? This is all about discovering your True Identity, and not relying on a lifelong assumption of who you *think* you are.

Can the appearance of changing form impact one iota of the change-less, formless identity You Are?

The belief in the "me," that fictitious center where everything is referenced to, is the cause of all your problems. Seen through as false, watch all your problems dissolve. Once the falsity of something is seen, you can never go back to believing in it.

What you no longer give life to cannot survive.

The false cannot stand up to examination – and what is true is what always remains. What is true stands alone and needs no defense, never crumbling even under the most scrutiny. Only the false needs defending. Only what is believed needs defending.

The ego is nothing other than a believed in thinking entity that moves towards pleasure and away from pain. There is no ego present anywhere; it's a phantom with no existence. Look for it and tell me where it is located.

When thought stops, where is ego?

When thought stops appearing, what remains?

Just an immediate, naked space of knowing remains – without any conceptualizing going on.

Ego is simply the movement of thoughts (thinking) towards objects of perception, in the form of grasping or aversion. It is an endless loop appearing in Consciousness and fools Consciousness into a trance of identification. It is "me" that doesn't like "this."

It is "me" that must have "that."

Thought (ego) has no independent nature. Just look. Does it exist by itself, apart from awareness?

All thinking comes and goes – and is witnessed and known. If it can be seen and known, it is appearance only, and can never leave a stain on what you are.

There is no need to grasp onto or avoid any experience, because the knowing of what it is all happening in is totally secure.

You Are Total Security Itself.

What are clouds, thunderstorms, tornadoes and hurricanes happening in? Don't they appear in a vast, empty, welcoming sky? The sky could care less how calm or nasty the weather is.

Before, during and after all kinds of weather, the sky remains unharmed and unconcerned.

You are the Un-manifest manifesting as everything – in the shape and form of a human being, in the shape and form of a thought, in the shape and form of a feeling, in the shape and form of an experience, and in the shape and form of all that is seen.

You are the Unseen that Sees all.

You are the one without a second, and while appearances appear to be separate, all appearances come from That – and are That. There is no separation between the seeing and the appearance being seen.

There is no division or separation in the infinite. You are the real that produces the unreal. You are the Unborn Noumenon, continually giving birth to all temporal phenomena.

Ramana Maharishi said, *"The world is illusory, only Brahman is real. Brahman is the world."*

All passing phenomenon is subject to time, with a beginning, middle and end. All appearances arise in timeless being, that which never began, and that which never ends.

This wide-open expanse of Freedom is the Great Unborn. The Buddha said: *"There is an unborn, an unmade, an uncreate. Were it not for this unborn, unmade and uncreate, there would be no release from the born, the made, the created."*

It is not that the unborn was created with the body and will die with the body. It is not that it lives on after the body dies, for it never entered the stream of time. It is prior to the born body, and remains when the body goes.

Knowing what you are, as Eckhart said, *"There is fusion without confusion."* When you are all that appears, without beginning or end, what is there to fear? What is there to avoid? What do you have to work out?

Our greatest fear is not the fear of death; it's the fear of life. It is the fear of truly living, of being alive and awake and undefended in this moment. We close off to, numb out to, and resist the "negative" experiences.

But life includes absolutely everything, not just the "positive" experiences.

Unless we include the whole lot, we suffer. We can't pick and choose what we experience. To be totally alive is to recognize that we cannot protect ourselves from any of it.

There is much to be seen in the wisdom of no escape.

To be clear, this message is not about denying any appearance that arises, including the appearance of the apparent separate individual.

To dance as the Cosmic Dancer you are, it still seems essential to honor and acknowledge the appearance of the Grand Illusory Orchestration.

In the end, it's all for You!

Recognizing your Original Nature, it is seen that everything is appearance only, happening within the ever-present backdrop of awareness you are.

It is only when we fuse with illusion do we become confused.

Knowing what you are, confusion can't arise.

Chapter 12
Present Before Thought

"If Truth isn't right where you are,
where else do you expect to find it?"

– Zen Saying

There is something here, right where you are, that is already free and untouched from 'me and my difficulties,' from 'me and my insecurities,' from 'me and my sadness,' and from 'me and my sense of success and failure.' There is something present before the seeming division of inside and outside, up and down, here and there.

It is present before thought; it is immediate and prior to all experience and identification. We can hear the words of the Zen Master who said, "When I heard the sound of the bell ringing, there was no I and there was no bell; there was just the ringing."

In other words, there wasn't anyone separate listening to the sound of a bell.

There was just immediate experience, prior to any commentary about it.

There was no listener.

Drop all concepts for a moment and pause all thinking. This is about looking and knowing for yourself, immediately in your own experience, what you are. Without referencing the mind, look right there, in that pause.

What can you say about it? Granted, it seems like nothing is there. To the mind it *is* no-thing.

It's not a cold and empty nothing, but a nothing so full, intimate and complete – beyond the comprehension of the mind.

The invitation is to stay with (and rest in) that no-thing for a while, without describing or labeling it. Is it scarred by any past dramas or traumas, or is it spacious, alive and peaceful? Does it come and go, or is it ever-present?

Staying away from concepts and labels, is it rejecting or resisting anything? Is it demanding anything be a certain way, or wishing anything were different than it is?

Just stay right here, right now, looking at the still, non-conceptual pause. Notice the silent, aware presence that never leaves – that everything comes and goes in. (That which comes and goes isn't real.)

That which is always present is real.

You are the Changeless Reality in which all change happens within.

If what you think you are changes (it does), it can't be real. Even if what you think you are never has changed, it still can't be what you are because you can never be what you *think* you are.

What you really are never comes or goes – and is prior to any conceptualization.

Therefore, YOU ARE REALITY, without condition or exception – As you are.

Might this still pause be the freedom and liberation you seek? Might you be the causeless joy, the peace that surpasses all understanding?

Yes, YOU ARE, as you are.

Why seek for what you already are?

Instead, why not be what you already are?

Because the ultimate reality isn't anything seen, but rather that which is Seeing, it doesn't matter at all what is being seen in any moment. Whether you see peace or conflict, calm or turbulence, happiness or sadness, matters not in the least; the Witnessing of these passing states is already free.

Changing states is not the point. Recognizing the always-present Seer is the whole point. Even in the most painful contractions, I have immediate and instant access to the ever-present Seer of those states, that which is eternally free of those states.

And so, it is not a matter of 'trying' to change my experience of these states, but instead, it is the simple acknowledgement that there is an untouched awareness present prior to thought and experience.

Resting in this pure and prior Witnessing, it is noticed that this Witnessing is not an experience that comes and goes, but is the vast and open expanse that allows all states to come and go in.

Resting in this simple Witnessing, I am no longer preoccupied in the search for particular experiences. I can let whatever comes, come.

None of it is a problem.

In truth, there is no Seer or Witness; there is simply Seeing, Witnessing – and You Are That. There is something that notices the silent seer or witness.

Like light, it cannot itself be seen, and yet it illuminates all that is seen.

We can't say it is absent, but it can never be found.

This is the mystery of being conscious.

We are ultimately never found, but obviously present and aware.

This is why it cannot be simply sensed; it must be realized. Being unable to speak about it directly, it is beyond language, beyond sense.

Whatever floats by my True Identity are like clouds floating by on a clear summer sky, and there is more than enough space in me for all of it.

The most sacred and the most profane are equally welcome in the Open Clearing I Am. The most extraordinary and ordinary are equally allowed in the space I am.

What I am never moves at all.

What I am is stillness itself, in which all things move.

Resting in this simple ever-present awareness, it is noticed that there is no inside versus an outside.

There is no subject versus an object.

Everything continues to unfold as it did before; birds still chirp, the sun still shines, babies still cry, the breeze still caresses the face, but there isn't anyone present to resist or cling to any of it.

All arises in the spacious and aware freedom that I am.

In my contracted state of the little me, I am 'in here' looking out at objects 'out there' – and this is the illusory divide that is the cause of all my problems.

Being on this side of my face that looks out, I am in constant protection mode, attempting to experience only that which I deem comfortable and pleasurable.

When it is seen that everything is simply vibrating energy in constant movement, you realize it's all a defense against nothing.

Resting in what I Really am, all that mental activity and resistance drops away in the thought-free expanse I am.

In seeing that inside and outside are mere mental constructs – and the primary reason for the struggle, all separation dissolves back into the boundless energy I am.

The sensation that once set me apart from all that was 'outside' fades into the nothingness from which it came.

Subject and object are no more. I no longer see the clouds – I am the clouds. I no longer see the sun shining – I am the sun shining. I no longer feel the breeze on my face – I am that breeze.

The clouds, sun and the cool breeze are within me; they are Me. The sun isn't an object seen 'out there,' but radiates deep within my being, shining everywhere all at once.

Resting in ever-present awareness, every object is its own subject. Every arising sees itself, for *I am that arising seeing itself.*

I am not looking at the moon; I am the moon that sees itself. I am not looking at the ocean; I am the ocean that sees itself.

Everything still goes on just as before, but in the absence of the subject and object split that divides, when there isn't any divide.

Thus, the tree is still a tree, but it's not an object being looked at, and I am not a separate subject looking at it. The tree and I simultaneously appear in the presence of awareness, already free in that expanse, arising as a non-dual movement, in a non-dual space.

This Spirit, this pure awareness is the one thing that never leaves. It is one constant that is always present in experience. It is the one constant in an ever-changing experience.

Seeing this, the separate self is seen through and is no more. Resting in the open expanse that I am, I stand absolutely free.

No thoughts, no words are needed to see what you are. In your own experience, see what you are, prior to words. You are present before thought.

No amount of translation is needed to see and be what you are.

It's already happening. See?

Chapter 13
Oh, What Webs We Weave

"Oh, what tangled webs we weave, when first we practice to deceive."
– Sir Walter Scott

If I had to sum up in one word the primary reason why the vast majority has yet to awaken to their true nature, I'd have to say, "Self-deception." Not only do we have it down pat – we're darn good at it. And we don't even know it. Deceiving ourselves in a variety of ways, we often get mired in illusion that inevitably hurts.

Because we don't set out to deceive ourselves, we have a difficult time recognizing how it happens. In order to come to some understanding, we sometimes conclude we're just at the 'wrong place at the wrong time.'

Unaware that we practice deception, in a trance-like state, we remain under its hypnotic spell. We pretend that what *isn't*, somehow, is far better than what *is*. We often pretend that what is, as it is, isn't what we want – when in fact, it can't be any other way.

We *pretend* that things can be different than they are, and in our desire for something different, we attempt to change what is. And since sometimes it works, it becomes a strategy, a way of orientation towards what is.

However, most times in our attempts to change what is, we suffer because resistance is present. In fact, the only problem we ever really have is when we want something other than what is arising. It really is that simple.

In this pretence, we forget that while things are often different than how they were – and even how they will be, they are never different than they are.

This 'how they are' is the 'what is' that is being referred to here. The mind has a difficult time accepting what is – and meeting what is, as it is. Always looking to make things better or different, it pretends what is, isn't enough, isn't satisfactory.

This belief keeps us on a never-ending journey towards happiness and enlightenment – and it ensures that we'll never reach a point of permanent and lasting fulfillment.

As long as the ego personality is focused on a journey in time towards something *other than what is*, it can successfully avoid what it fears most – it's own annihilation by Consciousness, that which the ego per-sonality appears in, and that which it is dependent upon.

Make no mistake about it, what the mind longs for and fears most at the same time is its own absence, its own disappearance as the captain steering the ship. When what *isn't* present is viewed to be more desir-able than what *is* present, the actual reality of the present moment is inwardly resisted.

This unquestioned belief is the fuel that drives the treadmill of suffering.

Trace back this contraction felt in the body to the belief that things can be different than they are. They never can.

Consciousness, the All That Is, can never be oversimplified. In fact, it is simplicity itself, while the mind is complexity itself. Indivisible Con-sciousness can only express itself in the illusory world of polarities by pretending to be divisible.

Remarkably, its fundamental nature is to be what it is by pretending to become what it's pretending to not be.

In Reality, Consciousness has no opposite and can't transform into what isn't. It is the only thing present, and always what is. Said differently, Reality is what is – and can never be what isn't.

So, whenever we pretend that there is something better than what is, we never actually experience the reality of the moment as it unfolds.

In our striving to make what is other than it is, the ego is protecting itself from being exposed as the phantom it is.

Deep down, the ego knows it's a fraud, but its fear of exposure trumps any desire to give up control; it doesn't want to see it has no control.

Ego, being just a thought, doesn't want to be seen through. It doesn't want to be served its walking papers. And as long as the search continues, as long as the belief that what is isn't enough, the searcher gets confirmation as being separate from that which he is searching for.

However, in truth, we can't ever get away from what we are, for we already *are* what we're trying to get away from. We can't ever escape where we are, for wherever we go, there we are. We already are where we are running to, even if we don't recognize it.

Consciousness revels joyously in all experience, no matter what occurs. It loves the entire play, as it is, and never avoids any of it. And it appears only to remember its Self-deception with a great deal of reluctance. Nobody, it seems, wants a good story to end.

For example, if you stand up in a middle of a riveting movie and turn on the lights and begin reminding everyone that it's just an illusion, that it's all made up, most will tell you sit down and shut up – and while you're at it, turn out those lights!

While we complain and wish things were better or different, secretly we relish in all the drama. Egos love drama. Egos love gossiping about other egos. Egos bond with other egos, through sad stories, comedic stories, happy stories and victim stories – but mostly through the not so pleasant stories. Have you noticed?

To be totally clear, these are just words that point to something else. None of these words are the actual, and only paint a picture in imagination, attempting to point to the actual.

There never are any actual webs we weave; there never is any actual separation – or anyone who is in or out of the flow of life. All perceived webs woven are nothing other than mental creations without any reality.

Even imagined problems and imagined identifications are none other than the Indivisible One showing up as divisive imaginary problems, in an imagined individual.

Nothing needs to be changed or fixed – ever.

You are Consciousness Itself, and you can't ever separate yourself from the Reality you already are. That would be as impossible as separating dryness from the desert, or wetness from water.

You are the Light that gives life to the movie of 'your' life, always.

Enlightenment, or the discovery of what you've always been, is never about something "out there." It's about clearly recognizing the essential Truth about what actually is, not what you think it is.

In the meantime, the drama will continue to unfold as it always does, however convincingly. The difference is that you don't believe it anymore. The mirage of water in the desert still looks like water even after the discovery it's just an illusion.

Finally awakening to the dream, the dreamer dissolves entirely back into that which can't be named.

Chapter 14
The Essence of What Is

*"Out beyond ideas of wrong-doing and right-doing, there is a field.
I'll meet you there. When the soul lies down in the grass, the world
is too full to talk about. Ideas, language, even the phrase 'each other'
doesn't make any sense."*

– Rumi

My Guru never leaves me. In fact, my Guru can't ever leave me, as
my Guru is this present moment. This moment, as it is, is the
True Teacher.

If spirituality can be said to be anything at all, it would have to be
about the essence of Reality, or the essence of what is. It has everything
to do with being awake to life as it unfolds. It has everything to do with
meeting what actually arises without any judgment or resistance.

It's about waking up from delusion, seeing through the stories of the
mind, dis-identifying with the cycle of avoiding pain and chasing after
pleasure as the chief aim in life.

Waking up has nothing to do with building character, self-improve-
ment or being the best person you can be. It has nothing to do with

'doing unto others as you would have them do unto you.' In the clear recognition of what you are, it is seen there is no "other."

Consequently, when it is seen that you *are* the so-called 'other,' you realize that what you do to 'others,' you in fact do to yourself.

So while you may hear that there is no right and wrong in Reality, because Reality is beyond the distinctions of right and wrong, there is, however, an ethic to enlightenment. Knowing it's all One, why would the One desire to harm itself?

Waking up to Reality is simply about being awake and aware to what is – being present to how life actually expresses, here and now. Here and now, as it is, is the only Reality – *before* the mind labels experience as good or bad, right or wrong.

While it seems mysterious, it is so unavoidably obvious.

It is the open secret that everyone is looking for, but can't ever find.

Thinking it must be complex, we get lost in complex thinking, when all along it's so radically simple. Identified with the thinking mind as who we are, we chase after all kinds of sensations and experiences, imagining that anything must be better than this. After all, the mind tells us so.

Everything is ultimately how it is. There's murder, there's rape, there's war, there's genocide – and everything else in between. The only time we suffer is when we think it shouldn't be that way. In my opinion, many 'teachers' have done the world a great disservice by pretending not to be touched by any of it.

In the end, it's not about whether you've been touched or not. It's how you deal with that touch. Either you're internally trying to control that touch, resist that touch – or you open and allow that experience to wash through you. In that allowing, there is no obstruction to the experience and it is felt without the filter of the mind.

It's all fundamentally sensation, coming and going. When you let all sensation be experienced without thinking it should be different, you notice an intimacy with experience, where before there was judgment and denial. When we label our sensations, we call them 'sadness,' 'fear' or 'anger' – and we make these sensations seemingly solid.

But nothing is ever solid; sensations are constantly in flux, moving in and out.

What defense is needed against something without solidity?

Being filtered through the mind with labels, we experience a sense of either desiring to push it away or trying to control it. There's a judgmental quality to it. And in this movement away – and in this wanting to control, we feel owned by the experience.

Conversely, if these sensations are allowed as they are, without labels, we let them move freely in us. In this way, they are allowed to move as they will move – and we no longer feel bound.

We meet this moment with all our "past knowledge" and superimpose it onto this fresh and new moment. In our unwillingness NOT to know in this moment, we compare what's arising with our databank of past stored knowledge. We project that data onto this new moment, but right now will never happen again exactly in this way.

We overlook what is so utterly obvious; we overlook what is actually present – the 'Isness' of the moment – and we latch onto the notion that "this isn't what I want" – and the search for some fantasy 'out there' is born of resistance to what is.

Allowing is not a 'doing' – it is the radically simple noticing that everything that appears in awareness is already allowed in, as it is. It could be the most joyous occasion to the most horrific tragedy.

So, there is no need to 'try' and allow, but simply see that this allowing has already happened in the vastness of what you are.

Nothing is denied entry.

Only the mind resists what is.

Life has a way of bringing us to our knees from time to time, whether it's through failure, great disappointment, abandonment, suffering, loss or utter exhaustion from seeking. The real question is whether we're on our knees praying to be delivered from what is, or are we on our knees, both in pain and surrender to what is already here.

Being present to what is without ever moving away from it, we recognize that it's very possible to be open to any kind of experience without crumbling inside, or feeling threatened. By simply being present to *whatever* arises, we see that when we don't resist any experience, the experience never owns us.

Nothing can ever threaten what we are.

Nothing can ever harm what we are.

And yet, there is no 'we.'

Anxiety, pain, frustration and confusion are no longer overwhelming or something to run from. We meet it without ever turning away from it. It's no longer feared because we see nothing is solid and nothing ever lasts. We notice that it was always worse in our minds than it actually is.

Allowing everything to be as it is, without the filter of the mind, nothing ever tortures us. Nothing *can* torture when all is welcomed.

Torture only happens when resistance is present.

Granted, we still have preferences, likes and dislikes. Humans have unique desires and preferences – and this it perfectly appropriate. However, while we maintain those preferences, we still have more than enough room for all of it because we know that what arises can't be any other way.

Reality is always what is, and never what we'd prefer it to be.

If something profoundly touches us, whether it is painful or joyous, we can simply *be* with it without trying to change or fix it. Being with it is not about changing it. Being with it is about meeting it, as it shows up, and how it shows up.

Being with what is brings you out of the mental realm of thinking and into the non-conceptual realm of sensory experience. No longer referencing thought to describe experience, any residual distance or separation dissolves. As a result, experience is felt directly, without an overlay.

While there is an aspect of us that can be touched by the pain, anger or fear, we never lose sight of what all those sensations are happening in. When the world may be falling apart all around us, we are firmly rooted in that which never falls apart. Sensations occurring in the body are allowed in the untouched reality of what we are.

The Primacy of Presence, that which isn't harmed, is utterly immediate – and what is, is experienced, firsthand.

And so, this is never about eliminating or changing anything. It's about being awake to what is – and not thinking what isn't is it. Instead, you're in the flow of what is and yet, there isn't a 'you' in the flow of what is. That's just more duality. There is just the flow of life – and you *are* this flow.

You need nothing to be happy; you need something to be sad. Unless you are fulfilled with nothing, nothing will fulfill you.

Awake to what is, there is no disillusioned or enlightened one to be found. There isn't anyone apart from That which appears as everything. There is no one present apart from the One that can always be this way or that way.

In this knowing, many of the same activities can still go on, but it's evident we aren't 'doing' any of it.

There is simply this inexpressible dance, as it is, in which nothing is excluded.

Your true teacher is this present moment, as it is.

Being with what is takes no effort at all.

Chapter 15
Thinking

"Subject-object thinking seems to cover the natural state of awareness. But without awareness, thinking could not take place. Because thinking appears in awareness – like clouds appear in the sky – realize that thinking is in essence awareness. Understanding this, thinking cannot obscure awareness."

– Bob Adamson

Most of us hang out in the mental realm all day long. Everything that goes on is filtered through the mind – "they like me, they don't like me, I like it, I don't like it."

For thirty-nine years I thought that "I" was the one doing the thinking. For many years, I thought "I" was the one who decided what to think, what not to think – and how to think. Reading books like "Change your thinking, change your life" or "What to say when you talk to yourself" only reinforced the illusion that there was a separate "I" who thinks.

And around and around the merry go round of suffering I went – for a long time.

Believing I was the thinker of thoughts, naturally I took ownership of the process and suffered deeply.

It wasn't until the deep recognition that thinking happens all by itself was I released from the notion of the one who was doing the thinking. It wasn't until seeing beyond all doubt that beliefs, opinions and judgments held in the mind were not of "my" doing, was I finally free from them.

Thinking happens, but is there a thinker? Don't we split it up between the thinker and the thought – as in, a thinker who thinks thoughts? Where is this thinker who thinks? Without referring to more thinking, is there a division actually present, or is it just something we've assumed for so long?

Can you find this division? If we see through the illusion that we are the mind (the thinker) that thinks thoughts, what must happen to the effects?

Identification with thinking drops away. Taking ownership of thinking drops away, for no one. No more suffering from thinking.

You don't have thoughts. You never did. You are not the thinker of thoughts. You never were. You are the wide-open space in which all thinking arises. You are the vast empty sky that all thought-clouds form, move and dissolve in.

If there isn't a separate entity doing the thinking, who or what is thinking? If there isn't a separate entity, we can cancel out a "thinker" up there in our head, can't we? And what are we left with? We're just left with the thinking, right? What is doing the thinking? The same intelligence-energy that is "doing" everything else is what is doing the thinking.

The reality is, we don't "think" thoughts. They arise and are witnessed by what you are, that which is prior to thinking. The Immaculate Misconception is that "we" are the ones thinking. We claim ownership of thinking and say, "I am thinking and these are my thoughts."

If you believe this, you believe you *are* the mind.

And this is the cause of ALL your problems.

When thought stops, there's no 'you.'

When the mind stops, unreality stops.

This primal belief, upon which all other beliefs are based, is that Consciousness or Awareness is located in the body. In this misconception, we shrink ourselves into a separate entity that resides in the body.

Consciousness contracts into a fragile and vulnerable entity – and we believe the thoughts in our head.

Consequently, the search for peace and happiness begins, when peace and happiness is already our true nature.

To be clear, this division doesn't actually take place. Consciousness seems to contract into a little me with all kinds of self-condemning thoughts, insecurities and problems. It is a powerful illusion that appears to divide and separate the Oneness of experience into two separate things.

Out springs the "me" that is separate from all that is not "me." In this apparent division, suffering is born.

In Reality, thinking is nothing other than an appearance in what you are. Like everything else, thinking is temporal – an appearance that is witnessed and known.

The mind is designed to divide the world and everyone in it into body, mind and soul, good and evil, right and wrong, and past, present and future. All these divisions are illusory and keep the dream alive.

There is no mind per se – there is only thought arising. When there is no thinking, there is no mind. There is no hearer; there is only hearing happening, effortlessly. There is no seer; there is only effortless seeing, without a subject-object division, happening by itself. There is no lover separate from The Beloved.

The "you" who you think you are isn't the thinker. Thinking happens by itself, within what you *really* are.

It's not about fighting the mind; it's about letting the mind continue as it does. What is discovered is that the mind can function very well getting you from one place to another, but it's no longer your primary way of experiencing the world any more.

When I take a look at thinking, I notice it arises spontaneously. It is so obvious and in plain view, yet it is easy to understand why most overlook it. The recognition of your total and complete freedom is closer than breathing, nearer than hands and feet. It is so close we miss it. It's so close to thinking (in fact, it's inseparable from it) that we get fused with it.

And confusion ensues.

You are the thought-free capacity where thinking occurs in.

As capacity, you are eternally unbounded – and already free.

The lazy man's way to enlightenment is simple. It takes no effort at all. Effortlessly noticing what is present, prior to the commentary of the mind, is all it really takes. Oh, losing your entire world, too.

Most people will never awaken to what they are simply because they are looking in the wrong direction.

Most people won't awaken because they will continue to insist that what is happening shouldn't be happening.

Most people won't awaken because they are stuck on the belief that they are the one doing the thinking, instead of noticing that thinking happens spontaneously, without 'them.' Most are deeply attached to their neurosis.

Identified as the author of thinking, people insist on trying to control or change their experience. They look to *get* something, whether it's a different experience, or a better experience. It's the 'anything but this' orientation that brings about discomfort. But awakening is completely beyond the notion of getting or changing anything.

Liberation is the seeing that "you" never thought a single thing, ever.

Since this seeing several years ago, there has been a total freedom from all psychological bondage. The same goes for any emotional bondage, too. It just can't happen anymore. Granted, pain can arise but it isn't owned or named. It can come up for a bit (and is allowed to be) and then it dissipates – back into nothing.

The same holds true for emotions. Like thinking, they are simply temporal appearances that come and go – within the silent, aware presence I am.

All is welcome Here.

Re-discovering that I am the aware presence that thinking arose in, no thought was ever a problem anymore. No amount of thinking – and no 'quality' of thinking could ever "get" this.

In seeing what I really am, the contracted energy in the dream of individuality dissolved into the boundless freedom that was always present.

Seeing that thinking happens spontaneously and without any conscious intent was as radically simple as seeing the heart was beating by itself, that breathing and seeing and hearing were all happening by itself.

Seeing that this was *never* about the mind – and that none of this was *ever* about the mind, no longer did I look to the mind to reference Truth or Reality.

I could just let the mind do its thing. It didn't matter anymore what the mind came up with. I was free from mind and emotion.

No effort or striving needed. No changing or improving needed.

It was always here, but went unrecognized. It was so simple the mind overlooked it. It was so simple the mind couldn't fathom it. Once something is seen to be false, the energy of belief drops away and the false dissolves.

Sharing this with You is my pleasure; reminding You of what You already know brings me great joy. And yet, it isn't "me" reminding "you." It is You reminding You of what You know, but have simply forgotten.

Remember, You allowed your Self to forget your Self, in order to remember your Self.

It really is this simple – and You designed it this way. Being the One, you created the mind to think dualistically, always dividing and distinguishing this from that. As Meister Eckhart said, *"All these distinctions happen within the space where distinction never gazed."*

What are the implications of this? What are the implications that "you" never thought a single thought, ever? What are the implications if all along, it was Life thinking through the body/mind you call "you?"

How does this impact your view of your "past?"

How does this alter the perception of who you are?

Chapter 16
One Without A Second

"When you make the two one, you enter the Kingdom of Heaven."

– Jesus

Comparing all the great religions of the world, it is discovered that at the heart of each religion is one simple proposition: that central to all sentient beings is the *One Awareness in all beings.*

Regardless of one's religious background or beliefs, what you find at the heart of that religion is the same Awareness.

Another essential discovery of all the great spiritual traditions throughout the ages, including Buddhism, Zen, Christianity, Judaism, Sufism and Hinduism, is that all experience isn't split into a perceiving subject known as "I," and a perceived object, *including* the world that is seen.

The apparent separate entity and the apparent separate world are understood to be mere concepts that are superimposed, or projected onto the reality of experience.

There are not two things, a seer and a seen, in our actual experience. The seer and the seen are of one single substance and that substance is our Self, Consciousness. All objects of perception are within Consciousness, are they not? Objects appear within what we are – including the body and the mind.

And so, we see all objects as our Self; we see all objects take the shape of the seeing to become the visual world, that takes the shape of hearing to become a sound, that takes the shape of tasting to become a taste, that takes the shape of smell to become a smell, that takes the shape of touching to become a texture.

And it never becomes anything other than itself. All experience and perception is none other than the One appearing as two.

Looking for this Reality, looking for the animating essence in every experience of the mind, body and world, we discover Consciousness at the root, a Knowing Presence of Awareness that never leaves. In fact, we can never deny the fact of being, the fact we know we are.

This understanding is often referred to as Non-duality or Advaita, and is the unchanging, uncompromising substratum all these traditions point to. While it can never be adequately expressed directly, Sages, Seers, Mystics and Poets utilize language to point to This Reality.

Oneness created the mind to divide and separate – to only think in dualistic terms of the opposites. Everything that arises does so dualistically. Although each arising has an opposite, the actual reality is Non-dual, or One appearing as two – without an opposite. Freedom is the transcendence of the polarities, at the same time including the polarities.

In *The Chandogya Upanishad*, Brahman, the Absolute Reality, the ultimate state of consciousness, is described in quite simple fashion: *the Absolute is "One without a second."* It makes no mention of One opposed to a second, One outside of a second, One beyond or above a second – only One without a second.

In other words, the Absolute Reality is that which has nothing apart from it – and nothing other to it.

This was expressed in Isaiah as *"I am the Lord, and there is nothing else."* Jesus also said in The Gospel of Saint Thomas: *"I am the Light that is above them all, I am the All, the All came forth from Me and the All attained to Me. Cleave a piece of wood, I am there; Lift up the stone and you will find Me there."*

The single One opposes the plural Many, while the Non-dual embraces both equally. Oneness is most dualistic, excluding its opposite of Many-ness. There couldn't be one without many. Without dualism, Oneness couldn't be.

However, one without a second means one without an opposite, not one opposed to many. Reality includes multiplicity *and* unity. It is the ground of all Being, appearing as both this and that, here and there, up and down.

As Ken Wilber explains, "It isn't that a 'part' of the Absolute is present everywhere and in everything – as in *pantheism* – for that would imply a boundary within the Absolute Reality, giving to each thing a different piece of the eternal pie.

Instead, the whole Absolute is completely present at all points of space and time, without boundary or division, for the obvious reason that you can't have a different infinite eternal at each point."

There is uniqueness and variety for sure. However, being one without a second, there isn't anyone "special" or more worthy than another. There is only the Formless Unseen One, appearing as all the many seen forms.

If you find yourself feeling insecure or superior to anyone else, whether it due to race, religion or station in life, it simply means you are ignorant to what you really are.

The peace and freedom longed for is about subtraction, not addition. As Jesus said, *"You must lose your life to save it."* This is what he meant by salvation.

What Christ was pointing to is when there's no longer anyone taking ownership of life, or anyone trying to possess or avoid any experience, life is no longer something to be denied or resisted, but rather, something to be celebrated and enjoyed.

Until we do, we forever remain on the wheel of suffering, running from this and chasing that.

When Christ said, "The meek shall inherit the earth," he meant that only those with a deep humility will see the true nature of reality and thus, enter the kingdom of God.

Jeff foster offers a metaphor in an attempt to describe one without a second, and it goes like this: Imagine a tiny balloon filled with air, floating in an infinite and eternal sea of air.

The balloon tells itself, 'I am an individual balloon and I live in a world of many, many other individual balloons. Everything I do and experience has to do with my achievements, my failures, my feelings, my relationships and my past and future. I am just a small piece of the whole, an itty-bitty piece of life.'

Who you think you are rummages around for crumbs, all the while being the entire cake.

Now what the balloon resists and dreads most is its own popping, in other words, its own demise. Its own demise, or popping, is seen to be the end of its existence in space and time – its loss of 'my life' and everything that was once 'mine.' In other words, 'my small piece of the whole' is no longer.

The balloon cannot see that its demise is freedom. It cannot see that upon popping, 'my small piece of the whole' simply erupts back into everything, and that 'my life' dissolves back into life itself.

Only then will it see that 'my life' was just an illusion, an appearance of the whole itself, never separate from anything else, including all the other so-called 'individual' balloons.

All along, there was only everything that is, and that the 'me' was simply an idea believed in. The 'me' was the reference point that created all the unnecessary suffering and drama.

Upon death, nothing was lost. Never possessing anything in the first place, losing anything isn't possible.

The good news is that seeing this doesn't have to wait until physical death, upon the balloon popping. It can occur right now. Only when you lose 'your' life, will you save it."

There is no one that dies.

Death is a concept, just like heaven and hell.

Upon the physical death of the body/mind, the discovery that what you've been looking for was always doing the looking is seen because it was always present.

Granted, this makes no sense to the mind, but no one needs to go to the nut house. However, I am not speaking to the mind. I am speaking to YOU, the presence prior to the mind, that which notices the mind thinking.

Tony Parsons says, *"Oneness plays the game of being two, asleep looking for oneness. When awakening happens, it is only the dropping away of taking two-ness seriously; that's all we're talking about here. This whole thing is as simple as this – all that's in the way of awakening is a false idea. It really is. It's a pretence that you've been conditioned to believe. And when the idea that you are two drops away, there is oneness."*

There is no one here speaking. This is simply You speaking to You, in an attempt to remind your Self of what You already know.

This is a message from your Self to your Self: Wake up from the mind. Wake up from the idea of the past and future and remember what you've always been and always will be.

You are the untouched presence of awareness (Spirit) that allows absolutely everything to be. You are the One.

The Absolute is the One without a second – and YOU ARE THAT ONE.

Wu-men said, *"Let subject and object be so one that the wind cannot pass between them."*

There is no *real* duality in non-duality.

Enlightenment is the sudden realization that non-duality, not duality, is the reality of our experience. Consciousness is not private and personal, but universal and impersonal, eternally.

Chapter 17
The Elusive Obvious

"There is no greater mystery than this, that we keep seeking reality though in fact we are reality. We think that there is something hiding reality and that this must be destroyed before reality can be gained. How ridiculous! A day will dawn when you will laugh at all your past efforts. That which will be the day you laugh is also here and now."

– Ramana Maharshi

Consider this. Imagine your life as a novel.

On each page of the novel, regardless of what's occurring in the story, and regardless of what the words are describing, behind the actual words there is the white paper.

What is taking the words in? Do you notice the Space that is taking the words in? What you are looking at is printed words; what you are looking out of is *Space* for them.

The paper is hardly ever noticed or appreciated, even though it is absolutely essential. After all, could there be words present if it were not for the paper?

If our attention were to be drawn to the white paper on which the words are written, we would experience the sensation of suddenly being aware of something we realize is so obvious that it needn't require attention. We have the familiar experience of something that we were already in fact aware of.

And yet, being suddenly aware of the paper as the most necessary component for the words written on it, our awareness of the paper seems to be a new experience. As a result, something feels different. No longer writing off the paper as something so obvious that it needs no attention, suddenly we have a whole new appreciation for the necessity of the paper.

When we return our attention to the words after having noticed the paper, do we lose sight of the paper? Do we not now see both, the apparent two, simultaneously as one? And didn't we already experience them as one, without ever realizing it?

The words in the story have no independent existence apart from the paper. In fact, every word written on the page is only made of paper. Isn't awareness itself not the support and substance in the same way the paper is the support and substance of every word, yet independent of the word?

Does anything need to be added to the paper in order to see the paper? Does anything need to be added to this present experience in order to be aware of the awareness that *is* its support and substance?

The vast majority who read books take for granted how essential the paper is to the words written on it. Likewise, most take for granted how essential awareness is to every thought, sensation, feeling and experience.

And generally, what we take for granted we overlook, don't we?

What is so simple and obvious seems hidden. In its total openness, it seems obscured. It is so close that it cannot be known as an object, and yet it is always known because it can't be negated.

Even though the paper knows it's the most vital thing that all else is dependent on, it doesn't need gratitude. It is whole and complete in itself, never needing to be lauded or stroked. It is total and absolute security itself – and it needs nothing to be secure.

What you really are is like the paper behind the words. You are not your life story, your achievements, your lack of achievements, your successes or failures, your behavior or personality. What you really are is That on which all is written.

You are not your personality, character, strengths, weaknesses, regrets and hopes, or what you believe yourself to be. You are life itself, the boundless energy of being, the all-encompassing, all-embracing Beloved in which the story of "your" life unfolds.

If it is all-encompassing, where must you go to find it?

If the Infinite Consciousness is all-encompassing, then it must be equally present in anger, fear and suffering.

It's natural to want to experience oneness in the calm of meditation, or in the beauty of the landscape, but it must also be immediately available in pain, boredom, struggle and resistance, too.

The paper of a book is never influenced by the story being written on it. The paper of a book remains absolutely untouched and unharmed by any twists and turns, no matter how joyous or traumatic the story can become.

The paper is present to simply hold and embrace whatever is written upon it. The paper doesn't try to reject or accept, but allows anything and everything to be as it is, without any demands or conditions.

There can be wonderful and happy celebrations going on, and there can be brutal and bloody battles going on. Continual birth and death goes on, along with all the other cycles of life, yet the paper behind it all, that which gives life to the words and stories, remains forever present, already and always whole in its entirety – everywhere.

The paper needs nothing at all. The paper sits back, silently watching the story unfold, while simultaneously recognizing it isn't apart from the story. Having no division or boundary anywhere but in the minds of the characters in the story, the paper isn't affected in the smallest way.

What is being described can be a comedic story, a sad story, a frightening story, a cruel story, a war story or a painful and arduous search for truth. To the paper, it's appropriate as it is – and in fact, cannot unfold any other way than it does.

No matter the storyline, the paper has no need to figure out or anticipate what might happen next. Fear doesn't arise for the paper, ever. The paper doesn't lament on past words, nor feel guilty and shamed about what already occurred. It doesn't wish, hope or desire for anything to be different than it is.

And the paper allows the characters to believe otherwise – and then feel the effects of that erroneous thinking. The paper allows delusion and the inevitable suffering that arises from it to go on, all the while welcoming the characters to see the true source of suffering.

The paper remains ever-present and unaffected.

All is well with the paper, no matter what goes on in the story. It's not that "all shall be well," because that implies some future time – when there isn't any future time. To the paper, all is well – now, eternally and without condition.

The paper is a lover of what is and enjoys whatever story appears on it. The paper knows that truth or reality doesn't explain everything, but that it is everything. Never being separate or apart from the words on the paper, there is nothing to control, fear, accept or reject.

If the main character in the novel suddenly dies, or experiences a slow, painful death, it's perfectly okay to the paper. Grief doesn't arise for the paper, for it sees that it is never over. The character may have felt they were coming to an end, but the paper itself isn't fooled by the appearance of death. It is beyond the necessary birth and death of the characters in the novel.

If the main character prefers to stick to his or her belief systems and faith in their God – it's not a problem for the paper. Why would it be?

If it weren't for the paper giving life to the main character in the story, things like faith and belief wouldn't even exist.

The paper, being all that is, never makes a demand, and never commands. It doesn't ever punish itself.

The paper doesn't seek to resolve or tackle any issues or questions about anything, for it knows it is the answer itself. It knows it's all just a story being played out – and it allows itself to pretend to not know itself, in order to remember itself once again.

Even if the main character in the story dies before remembering, it's not even remotely problematic for the paper.

Upon death of the character, an instantaneous recognition of what it always has been occurs.

The paper welcomes all of it while making no demands on anything, anytime.

This is the greatest novel in existence – and it is what you've always been.

It's so elusively obvious and ever-present that the mind overlooks it.

It is so openly spacious that everything is contained within it.

It is so intimate that every experience, however small or vast, is saturated and permeated with its presence.

It is so unconditional and welcoming, that absolutely every experience is allowed as it is.

It is the Great Unknown that the known appears in.

It's already all that is. It is the fundamental essence that everything appears in, and is the destiny of all experience.

What already is cannot be attained. What already is needs no path or journey in time to realize.

YOU are the background of Space from which life's happenings appear in.

Chapter 18
The Answer Isn't In Thought

"Stop all delays, all seeking and striving. Put down your concepts, beliefs and ideas. For one instant, be still and directly encounter the silent unknown core of your being. In that instant, Freedom will embrace you and reveal the Awakening you are."

– Adyashanti

Undoubtedly you, the reader, are intelligent – and perhaps have been seeking for many years to find out what you are, what truth is. The mind is very useful for many things, but when it comes to discovering *This That You Are*, it's not the right tool for the job. It's like using a saw to hammer two pieces of wood together.

None of your 'knowledge' has brought you to the realization that You are the One that is looking through your eyes right now. Your 'knowledge' has not brought you relief from the pain and suffering that continues to frustrate you because of your ongoing belief in who you think you are.

Wisdom blooms when you finally see that all your knowledge hasn't delivered what you've been seeking.

Wisdom blooms when you recognize you can never be what you think you are.

The mind works in time – and in a linear fashion. It will turn anything into a dogma, and turn it into a process in time, believing the words to be the real. And those words end up torturing us, keeping us bound in time and caught between the polarities of good and bad, right and wrong, love and hate, rich and poor, worthy and unworthy, holy and unholy.

Because the unknowable Mystery that you are isn't an object in consciousness, your mind has little interest. If it can't be seen or known, the mind overlooks it. Mind looks in the direction of sensations, concepts and experiences when looking for *This* – and it never finds.

Using thought to recognize what you are is paramount to looking in the wrong direction. It's like facing east when you wish to watch the sun set. The Unknown, the invisible no-thing you are, can never be known by the mind, a thing.

To the mind, awareness is no-thing. It is without quality, attribute, shape, form, time or age. Awareness is clear and empty, yet it is the container in which all qualities, attributes, shapes and forms appear in.

The mind can't grasp or understand no-thing. The mind, being a "thing" in awareness, is dualistic in that it can only think in terms of opposites. It continually divides, condemns, resists and evaluates absolutely everything based on familiar and associative patterns based on the past.

How can the thinking mind, which can only think dualistically, apprehend the non-dual that it is cradled in? It can only bow to its source in silence.

You are the Non-dual Space of Awareness that embraces all duality. You are the Non-dual Absolute that all duality arises in.

The mind, being a finite "thing" can never apprehend the infinite no-thing, the infinite that cradles all of existence, eternally. The mind can never grasp or understand what is prior to it.

Mind doesn't realize *This* cannot be approached with thought, but keeps looking anyway. It doesn't occur to the mind that perhaps it isn't found within its domain.

YOU know this already.

Thought (thinking) happens within the changeless presence of awareness that you are. Without you, awareness, thinking could not arise. Consequently, thinking has no independent existence apart from the awareness it arises in.

Apart from thinking, what mind is there? Where is it? Might the mind just be a concept, like the "me" thought? Look for yourself and don't assume or believe. What does present evidence reveal?

Like belief, imagination and desire, thought is an object in awareness that comes and goes. If it can be seen, it is an object. If it can be known, it must be an object. This is why what you ARE can never be known.

Can the eye see itself?

Can the sword cut itself?

If you could "know" what you are, you'd have to be an object. You are the Subject that contains all objects, including thinking. Being the One without a second, You are the objects that appear as well.

What you are encompasses the mind and therefore, the mind will never see that which contains it – and that which produced it.

If Truth is always present prior to thought, what need is there to reference thought for Truth or Reality?

It can never be what you *think* it is because this recognition isn't found in time or thought, nor can it be approached by thought. You are prior to thought – and that which contains thought. This is only discovered or realized in the timeless present.

The very notion there is something to seek and someone to seek implies time, and since mind lives in time, it won't ever be found. What you are, timeless presence of being, is *prior to and beyond* the mind, yet simultaneously envelops the mind that looks for it.

It is a futile search, always.

As Saint Francis of Assisi put it, *"What you're looking for is what's looking."*

You cannot look for this because it is doing the looking. You cannot see this precisely because it is doing the seeing. You cannot find this precisely because only an object can be found; you cannot find this because it is doing the finding.

If it is witnessed and known, it must be a "thing." A thing is an object. If it can't be seen or known, it is no-thing. Therefore, thinking is an object in awareness. See that it is not the mind that is aware of the mind thinking.

Seeing is not a matter of thinking.

Your True Nature is not an object that can be known by the five senses.

This is the reason you hear or read the words, "You are not who you think you are" and "Enlightenment isn't what you think it is."

The answer isn't in thought. You are prior to thought and contain all thought.

Chapter 19
I Am

"The only truth is I AM – I exist. That is the only truth. Everything else is a concept. Rebirth is a concept. Your karma is a concept."

– Ramesh Balsekar

When I discard all that is false, I am left with what I Am. In the midst of the false, I am.

I am the false in the True. I am the True in the false.

I am that which the mind will never comprehend.

I Am, exactly as I Am, an eternal expression of the infinite source of all that appears and disappears. You are the same eternal expression of the One Source, exactly as you are, right here and right now.

The Absolute isn't waiting for you to measure up to its standards. It has no concept of worthiness, yet is the container for such thoughts to appear in.

No purification, surrender or devotion is requisite. I am no more or less worthy or special than anyone else. If Oneness is all there is, how could I be more or less worthy than anyone else?

There isn't anyone else.

Oneness can have no hierarchy, levels or any separation at all. If oneness is all there is, then volition and free will are totally illusory, too. Choices are made, but there isn't any chooser.

I am the animating essence behind absolutely everything, including the appearance of a separate individual that appears to live in this world.

I am life happening – and since nothing can be excluded, all that appears is what I am. There are no more boundaries, but concepts of boundaries still appear in what I am.

I am not living "my" life. I am being lived by the One Life. There's nobody home here but a welcoming presence. This presence appears to be personal, but it's impersonal. What I really am – and not what I appear to be, is a lover of what is, not a lover of what could be.

Nothing needs to happen or change for me to be what I already am. I am the Source of wholeness itself, temporarily appearing in the form of a human being, non-separate from anything at all, here to express and enjoy what I am – the inexpressible, infinite All That Is.

I am not my mind, my body, my feelings or my experiences. I am not my life story, nor am I an image of myself. I am the boundless aliveness that is both empty and full at the same time. I am that which transcends and includes absolutely everything, never divided, only united.

I am the no-thing that is everything, and nothing is more sacred or holier than what I am. All is an equal expression of that which I Am. I don't own anything, nor do I identify with anything – even what I Am.

You can't find me, but there is no place that I am not. I am freedom itself, the silent aware presence that allows existence to be. I am the freedom that everyone is looking for.

I don't live in this world, nor do I 'have' a world. The world is within what I am. The seen world is simply a manifestation of what I am, forever coming and going.

There is no timeless now *and* what I am. That's just more dualistic thinking. Aware of time, I *am* the timeless now.

Aware of color, I am colorless.

Aware of thoughts, I am thoughtless.

Absolutely everything is occurring within what I am, eternally arising from – and falling back into – the empty, awake, welcoming space that I Am.

What is born must die. I was never born. I will never die. This body and mind will inevitably perish, but it is not what I Am.

There is only Source appearing, the one appearing as two, the no-thing appearing as everything. I am the Timeless, Impersonal Source that appears as the apparent personal in time.

I am That Which Cannot Be Named; I am the unchanging, still Source where constant change happens within.

I am the Absolute Emptiness in which the mind and all appearance collapses in, and then projects itself, within itself, back into the world of objective phenomenon.

I am completely vulnerable, but I am unharmed.

I am absolutely defenseless, but I am your refuge.

I am always present, but can't ever be approached.

I am uncaring for the sake of kindness.

I am aloof for the sake of intimacy.

I am ugly for the sake of beauty.

I am the thinking in the thought.

I am the feeling in the felt.

I am the seeing in the seen.

I am the touching in the touched.

I am the hearing in the heard.

I am the smelling in the smelled.

I am the tasting in the tasted.

I am not a "part of" the One – I Am the One.

What I am, you are.

I am.

Chapter 20
Dancing By Itself

"The whole world is an ever-changing state. No form is permanent. All you have to do is see the dream as a dream. You are the formless, timeless, unborn. I ask you to stop imagining that you were born, have parents, are a body, will die and so on."

– Nisargadatta Maharaj

If we simply look and notice what's already going on, we see that absolutely everything is changing. It doesn't matter if we're the least intelligent person on the planet, or the most intelligent person on the planet. We can all agree that everything changes, and that nothing remains the same.

If every "thing" is changing, then we can also agree that all of existence has no real form. If it changes, it can't have any solidity to it.

If no-thing has any form, we can't say what it is, either. We can imagine, assume, opine or believe, but descriptions can only inadequately describe the indescribable. Thus, we're destined to be lost in translation, that is, unless we see "things" for what they really are.

What we *can* say, however, is that all of existence is an indescribable, immeasurable, changing, formless dance – and not a conglomeration of definable, measurable, static forms that remain. Granted, some things change slowly that we don't notice unless we access our memory of its original state.

Thoughts appear and disappear, all by themselves. Memories, images, ideas and sensations present themselves in awareness spontaneously, linger for a bit and then disappear back from where they came. Sounds arise out of nowhere – a doorbell ringing, a car skidding, a dog barking, a bird chirping and a cat meowing.

Stories of what should have been done in the past, as well as stories about what could be done in the future appear out of nowhere, are felt and experienced for a bit, only to subside back into where they came from – like a wave in the vast ocean of awareness you are.

All kinds of feelings come and go – boredom, frustration, anger, happiness and sadness.

What witnesses all this never comes and goes.

Trees, houses, cars, oceans, rivers and mountains all change, however slowly. Beliefs, assumptions and opinions can seem unchanging, but in the end, they too, tend to change often. Thoughts, moods, perceptions and behaviors tend to change rather quickly and subsequently, are more easily noticed as that which changes.

The tides coming and going, the seasons changing, the migration of the birds headed south for the winter, stars exploding and black holes forming in the furthest galaxies all suggest that existence is an intelligent, moving, shifting, vibrating, continuous happening.

No matter how seemingly significant or insignificant, everything is constantly changing – and everything arises spontaneously in the Unchanging Awareness you are.

Bringing your attention to this moment, what do you find? What is happening? Do you find a fixed, unchanging, solid entity called "you" present – or do you find that everything is in constant flux, changing from moment to moment?

Do you see any solidity, or do you see a never-ending dance of movement in the form of thinking, feeling, sensation and experience?

Can it be seen that the formless dance happens by itself? Can it be seen that all appearance and experience happens in the vast, open space you are?

If we simply notice what is going on in our direct experience, we can feel the heart beating and the lungs breathing. We notice the eyes already seeing and the ears already hearing. We can witness the mind alternating back and forth between thinking and silence.

We can notice we don't decide when to think, or what to think.

We can notice decisions and actions happening all by themselves.

We see it all happens by itself – it's One Cosmic Dance.

Is there a dancer doing the dance, or is there only the dance?

Have you ever *really* looked?

All manifestation is often said to be the play of Consciousness – or *Lila*. Only Consciousness is truly present, and its magnificent nature is to pretend it's not pretending.

It is apparent that you are compelled to dance out your part of the Divine play, until you awaken to the discovery that there's never been any difference between you as the Dancer and you as the Dance.

If you are the one in control of your thinking, why don't you just stop thinking for a day? Too long, you say? Okay, let's make it much simpler. You're in control, so stop thinking for ten minutes. How far will you get? A few seconds, maybe? That's it? And you claim you are directing your life?

How can you say that with a straight face? Ha!

If you choose your thoughts, why would you ever choose negative, self-defeating thoughts? If you choose your thoughts, you'd always choose happy and loving thoughts, wouldn't you? Since I don't choose my thoughts, I don't choose my decisions, either.

Therefore, I am not the doer.

It happens all by itself.

Most people, if they *really* look, can admit that thinking happens all by itself – and that they don't choose their thoughts, but will have a very difficult time seeing that they don't make decisions. To admit this would be to admit they have no control. And the mind is all about control.

Since the mind can't fathom this, it concludes that things would fall apart. It concludes that in order to live a 'balanced' life, it needs to be in control of its environment. Nothing could be further from the truth.

In fact, Life continues as it always has, but in the absence of a believed in separate entity pulling the strings.

The reality is Life is so much more capable of handling things than 'you' will ever be. Life is so much wiser than 'you' will ever be.

When thinking ceases, does Life fall apart?

Choices are made, but there isn't a chooser. Decisions are made, but there isn't a decider. Thinking happens, but there is no thinker. Seeing happens, but there is no seer. Hearing happens, but there is no hearer. Smelling happens, but there is no smeller.

You don't make cells in your body die and you don't grow new ones. You don't fire all that electrical energy in your brain, nor do you decide when insights arise – let alone what kind of insight. You don't make blood flow throughout your veins, nor do you choose when your last breath may be.

It happens all by itself.

You don't make your hair grow, your skin and body age, nor do you ever decide to have a particular feeling. You don't decide when to feel anger, love, fear, courage, happiness or sadness. Feelings spontaneously emerge within the feeling-less space you are, without your intent.

Did you decide what kind of music you like, or does it just happen? Did you decide on what kinds of foods you enjoy, or does it just happen? Would you decide to help an old lady who fell on the sidewalk, or would it just happen?

If we got to decide on our strengths, weaknesses and intellectual capacity, no doubt we would have a planet full of highly intelligent, highly capable renaissance men and women, painting Picassos, writing like Twain and creating music like Mozart. But none of this is the case – and it never was.

No amount of wishing, desiring, comparing, envy or jealously will ever transform us into what we're not. Seeing it's all a spontaneous dance, all desire to change anything drops away …

And we meet what is, as it is.

Life becomes a miracle as soon as it is seen that Consciousness is not personal but universal. Life becomes more like a symphony with an endless crescendo, dancing as the appearance of a separate person going somewhere.

While there is still an apparent individual thinking defeating thoughts, happy thoughts, the melody plays on, uninterrupted and unconcerned.

The divine manifestation expresses itself through a daydream that looks and feels personal – and this daydream needs an empty backdrop, an empty Space, a Space that is impersonal. An eternal cycle of creation and destruction plays out. Nothing is ever really destroyed; it's just transformed and reconstituted.

Are we really a collection of thoughts, feelings, perceptions and experiences that constantly appear and disappear – or are we the vast and open expanse that all these things come and go in?

Once it is seen that there is no personal entity, personal thoughts have no solid ground to stand on. You see them for what they are, vibrations of energy inseparable from the Awareness you are.

Feelings may still arise, but we don't label or turn them into thoughts. Like bubbles in boiling water, they come up, but when the source of the heat is gone, they dissolve back into where they came from.

If we look a bit closer, we see that none of it is of our own conscious doing – and that it never was – and that all of it is simply a spontaneous dance unfolding all on its own.

Just as you didn't get to decide who your parents are, you didn't get to decide on your particular set of wants, needs and desires, either. We don't create what we want to do, need to do, or capable to do.

Conversely, we don't decide on what we don't want, don't need and aren't capable of.

You have never 'done' anything in life. Yet we pretend we are the one pulling our own strings. We pretend to be the captain of our own ship. The mind fears seeing this, but You don't.

All the while a non-dual happening unfolds dualistically. It's one formless dance, appearing to play the game of two, effortlessly unfolding as the ever-changing aliveness of this moment.

The only thing that doesn't change witnesses all of it coming and going. The one constant throughout is the ever-present witnessing aware-ness that you are, that which everything emerges from and returns to.

You are the untouched and unchanging, where the entire dance spontaneously happens within.

Simultaneously, you are the Dance, too.

Chapter 21
A Center-less Center

"Why are you unhappy? Because 99% of everything you think, and everything you do, is for your self – and there isn't one."

– Wei Wu Wei

The Absolute, as Saint Bonaventure put it, is *"A sphere, whose center is everywhere and whose circumference nowhere,"* meaning that while it is nowhere, nowhere is it not. Being nowhere, it is everywhere.

To the dualistic mind, this is pure lunacy – and those who speak of such things ought to be locked up. Nonetheless, there are way more insane people outside of institutions than there are inside them. It's not even close.

The reason the Absolute can be entirely present at every point in space and time is because *It* is *without* space and time. Being timeless and space-less, it contains and embraces all space and time. Being time-less and space-less, it doesn't have to contend with space, and is eternally free to contain both.

It's like water, being without shape and form, fills containers of every shape and form.

So many intelligent people of all faiths and traditions will agree that the Absolute, God, Reality, Truth or whatever you prefer to call it is everywhere all the time, but then have a hard time believing they *are* the Source of Everything. They find it very difficult to wrap their heads around this.

And it makes perfect sense because the mind can't understand or grasp the infinite.

You can't *believe* you are the Source. You can, but it doesn't mean anything, because you don't know it. In other words, there won't be any lasting byproducts (or fruits) from that belief. You can only *realize* you are the Source.

Belief is of the mind and realization is of the heart, or Spirit, that you are.

And so, the difficulty with telling someone they ARE the Source is that the mind will hear that and think that they, as a separate individual, ARE the source. However, this has nothing to do with individuality. This has nothing to do with the "me."

This message is for That which is beyond the mind. You know this already. This isn't "me" writing to "you." Again, this is YOU sending a message to your Self, reminding YOU of what YOU already know, but have simply forgotten. There is no "you" sitting there reading what "I" have written.

For many, just the thought of this realization would really mess with things. It would mess with their idea of their God, their purpose in life, the meaning they give to their lives and where they're headed in the afterlife.

The whole house of cards would collapse – and they sense it, so they don't look for themselves. They don't want to see its all a complete fabrication, albeit, a seemingly real fabrication.

How many people want to see that they are Mr. or Mrs. Nobody with no real purpose or meaning other than to awaken to the dream?

Naturally, all this speculation happens before realization. Upon realization, all that was invested in won't be cared about anymore.

You would think that most would be eager to discover they are what they've been seeking all along. You would think most would be eager to discover that what they are is ALL they see, without separation, condition or requirement.

Not so.

Many get stuck on and worship the messenger instead of putting their attention on the message. It's like worshipping and bowing down to the finger instead of looking to what the finger is pointing to.

Not many want to lose their life in order to save it, especially those who have a relatively happy life, fulfilling most of their wants, needs and desires. Most that live a 'pretty good life' are content with the status quo. A comfortable dream is much more acceptable than a nightmare.

Either way, there aren't many who want to lose their life in order to save it – especially *just in case* Jesus, Muhammad and Allah really are the Messiah! Sorry, I couldn't resist.

Saint Paul used to say, *"I die daily."* Saint Francis of Assisi said, *"It is only by dying that I can have eternal life."* These men weren't talking about physical death. They were talking about the fictitious self-center most believe themselves to be. They were talking about dying to the beliefs and concepts most take to be real.

Let's take a different angle here.

What is the body made of? Like earth, it's made up of over 75% water and all the elements in nature, is it not? There is air, space, matter and fire. All these elements can be broken down into particles the human eyes can't see. There are atoms, wave particles and quarks – and it's basically just energy vibrating at a certain frequency.

The body is made of the elements, just like everything else.

All form (matter) is essentially vibrating energy, flashing in and out of existence so fast the senses can't pick it up. In fact, matter has never been found. Nothing is solid, although it appears and feels solid. The earth is spinning so fast on its axis that the senses can't notice.

It appears still, but it's anything *but* still.

All forms are formless, while appearing solid.

The body isn't separate from the elements; it is made of the elements. How would the body hold up without water? How would the body fare without space and body heat? Could it walk and talk and function if it wasn't in the appearance of matter? You'd be a ghost if it weren't for the appearance of matter.

The body would be dead without being in unison with all of these elements. The body cannot be separate from the elements, just as the mind can't be separate from the illusory world it sees and believes in.

The same source intelligence-energy that drives the entire universe, the earth to rotate on its axis, that placed the sun at the right distance from the earth to support life, is the very same intelligence that is beating your heart right now, breathing through your lungs right now, growing your hair and fingernails – and seeing through your eyes right now.

You think "you" are looking out through your eyes right now. You think it's "you," the body/mind with a personality, name, birthday, family history, age, gender and eventual death date, that is looking through your eyes right now.

That sense of it being "you" is simply pure being, that raw alive energy that never goes away, that never dies. You've thought it was "you," but it isn't who you are; it's what you are.

You are the presence, the intelligence-energy that allows existence to be.

All there is is timeless being, and the idea of "you existing" arises in that being. It is just a thought, a belief that's been reinforced for so long.

If everything is within your awareness, can the moon be external to you? Without referring to thought, in your own direct experience, can anything at all be external to you? Is there anything outside of your consciousness? Everything is within your consciousness, isn't it?

Nothing is external to what you really are.

Now, if you identify who you are *as* the mind, that thing that will die someday, then naturally, you'll believe everything is external to you except for the thoughts in your head. But you can never prove it because it isn't so.

Are you located everywhere inside of the lining of your skin? Is that the dividing line you call *real* – where you end and everything else begins? Have you concluded that everything within the lining of your skin is called "me" and everything outside is called "other," or "not me?"

Look for yourself.

Trust in Being. Trust that Being isn't sending you on a wild goose chase. In order to keep looking, instead of tossing this out as pure folly, the invitation is to suspend your judgments and trust in the possibility that this author – which is none other than YOU – isn't coming from belief, opinion or conviction.

That said, never take my word – or anyone else's word; you must look and confirm for yourself.

STOP. Stop reading for a moment and simply look.

Are you looking?

If you are absolutely honest when looking – and earnestly desire to see what's really so, you'll find that all there is, is just space. There is no one there when you look. There's just an aware Space in which everything happens, in which everything arises in and falls back into.

No one who has ever really looked (in a non-conceptual way) has ever located the "me" they always assumed was present. All they can do is come up with a bunch of concepts and beliefs about who they think they are. And I'm going to go out on a limb here and guess you didn't find "you," either.

In your actual experience before thought, can you negate this non-finding?

Isn't the only appropriate and honest thing you *can* say, without referring to belief or thought is, "There's just an empty and vast aware Space in which all things are apparently happening in?"

Direct your attention to that aliveness that never leaves, that knowing presence of awareness that has never aged or changed since you were a small child. There is a dimension in you that has never aged, changed, or been stained over the years. It's the same now as it was then – and yet, there is no 'now and then.'

Does it have a gender, race or sexuality?

Does it have any qualities, characteristics or attributes?

Yet you recognize the fact of your own being, prior to all thought and sensation, don't you?

Can you *still* get a sense of moving behind the *appearance* of that guy or gal who's been around for a while, the guy or gal with attributes and qualities, an age, sexual orientation and race, with all the successes and failures – and all the happy and sad times?

And just behind that *appearance* of that guy or gal who's been around for a while is the one who *knows* that guy or gal. You know this; you *know* that there's something just behind, don't you?

You *know* there's something just behind "you," silently watching "you" sitting there and reading this – don't you?

Look without conceptualizing.

Disregard belief, assumption and opinion for a moment and look in your actual experience and tell me what you see? Remember not to use any words, assumptions or beliefs.

Can you find a solid entity called "you" – or do you find just a silent, aware presence, without any form and name? If you can't find "you," do you think that it's a gigantic, unwarranted leap to recognize that You are the Timeless, Nameless, Formless Being that allows all names and forms to appear and disappear in?

If "you" think "you" are contained within the lining of "your" skin, how is it possible to get a sense that there is something just behind "you," silently watching "you" – perhaps in confusion right now, or in peaceful delight right now?

Don't you get a sense of this? Don't you get a *real knowing sense* – and not just a *believed in, 'well maybe'* sense?

It may be disorienting and confusing at first, but so what? Is the awareness OF confusion confused? Is the awareness OF disorientation disoriented? What are feelings anyway? Feelings are simply vibrating energy – energy in motion – coming and going within the ever-present, unchanging being that you are.

If they can be seen, can they be real? If they can be known, can they be real?

Of course it's scary to the mind – who you think you are. It's like when you fell in love – and you 'lost yourself' – and it freaked you out. Having no center, you feared losing control. You disappeared. You may have even backed off a bit and took it slower, all in an effort to regain control – and your "identity" back.

The funny thing is, you have no identity – and you have no control. You just believe you do because it appears (and feels as if) you do – and you've been taught since childhood that you have an identity and you have control. Identity and control are both illusory concepts taken to be real, just like the mirage in the desert is taken to be real.

The "you" was never in control over any of it anyway, because it was never present in the first place. It was simply imagined. If Life lives Itself, through you and as you, who is present to exercise any control?

Can an illusion wake up? Can an imagined self awaken?

No, it cannot.

The feeling of losing the imagined center in relationship can range from liberating to totally horrific. Losing the imagined center out in nature tends to be a different story. The experience is usually very peaceful and liberating.

Not many get self-conscious and insecure amongst the wonder and beauty of nature.

Union typically happens, and yet, there was never any division in the first place.

The loss of the imagined center in relationship happened here a few times in my twenties. It was very uncomfortable, indeed.

Looking back, it was simply The Universal Beloved in Love with itself, dissolving back into Itself, without any imagined boundary or division. In that experience, the contracted energy of "me" took a short vacation, dissolving back into the boundless energy of freedom and release.

At first, it feels so free and wonderful, but as time goes on, the "me" inevitably reinserts itself back into the picture and says, "Whoa, what about me? What happened – and where'd I go?"

The experience of no center is not at all attractive to the "you" you think you are – and that idea of "you" will do whatever it takes to regain control, even at the expense of that wonderful, spacious feeling.

The mind, thinking it's the one pulling the strings, fears it won't be in control – and will do anything it can to postpone this seeing.

YOU designed it this way. There is nothing wrong with this.

The mind will do whatever it can to remain in control. The mind is all about its own survival. But remember, this isn't about the mind. Seen for what it really is, the mind can do its thing; it's not a threat or an obstacle.

The mind doesn't want to see that it's really not behind the steering wheel directing a life. In fact, it fears seeing this.

As Jesus said, *"The birds in the sky have their nests; the foxes have their holes in the ground, but the son of man has nowhere to rest his head."*

This is precisely the center-less center Jesus was pointing to.

You are the center-less center, the alive energy of Being that all imagined "me's" appear in.

Chapter 22
Nothing Personal

"Cease overlooking this terribly neglected spot, this center-point of our life, which on inspection instantly explodes into the universe, and all will come clear."

– Douglass Harding

If you start with the only thing you can be absolutely certain of, the fact of your own being is a great place to start. It's always present, never coming or going.

Is there ever a time you can say you are not?

You *know* that you are, and you say, "I am," but the thought "I am" is not the reality – it's merely a thought, a concept. The am-ness is the real; the "I" is imagined.

What it's expressing is that sense of *knowing aware presence* you're absolutely certain of. That absolute knowing that you are is being expressed through the mind as the thought, "I am." Identification with this "I" thought is the cause of all your problems.

You've assumed it all your life – that your real identity is this "I" that everything happens to. You probably never really looked deeply into it; you just believe it, right? We've been taught this, haven't we? At birth, you're given a name, social security number and told, "You are a person."

Before about the age of two, there isn't any self-awareness. If your parents never put you in front of a mirror, you wouldn't be able to recognize the form staring back at you as you.

What is required is the seeing that there is no one home, no-body going anywhere. To the mind, this is about as enticing as taking a walk in the park on a below freezing day, without the proper clothing. But this isn't about the mind, nor is this for the mind.

It is well worth repeating: Enlightenment and Liberation has nothing to do with the mind – and it has nothing to do with you.

Does this mean to just be a couch potato and do nothing with your life? If I'm not doing anything, why bother with anything? Is there an implication here that says not to help the suffering of the world, or be an activist for change? No, it doesn't.

It simply means that all this can still go on, but for no one. When you no longer serve from a divisive attitude of what "should" or "must" be done, real change and healing occurs. Otherwise, you're just pumping more division into what you don't want, and giving more life to what you don't want.

If you want peace, be peace.

If you want love, be love.

There is no "should" or "must" in Reality, save the one the mind imposes. Real service happens in the absence of inner division. Bringing more division to an already divisive issue doesn't serve anyone.

Free from judgment and resistance, real service and healing activity happens. Enlightened action is the absence of anyone doing anything. *"Enlightened action leaves no trace."*

Almost every spiritual tradition tells us that God, Truth or Reality is omnipresent, omniscient and omnipotent. They all say it's fresh, non-conceptual, non-dual, ever-present, all-knowing and all-powerful.

Omni means all the time and everywhere – outside the stream of time – never coming, never going, and shining of its own accord. If it's everywhere all the time, where is there space for anything personal? "All" is that, without exception or condition.

This is why you hear what you are seeking you already are.

You can't *know* you are a separate person. You can fool yourself into thinking you know it, but it's just a belief that has gone unquestioned and examined. We were paraded in front of a mirror as a baby hearing, "Who is that? That's Mimi or that's Cathy. "

We learn to believe that who we are is that body staring back at us.

We aren't reminded early on that what we really are is that which is peering through the eyes of the baby called "Mimi" and "Cathy," and it is the Same Eye that peers through the eyes of ALL sentient beings. Don't we stop at appearances and say, "That's what we are?"

And don't we split the seeing up into three separate movements and say, "I see the sight?" We say, "I am seeing (the sight of) the moon," as if there is a real boundary between the "I" that *sees* the moon.

Look deeply at the next bright moon, alone and in silence – and without reference to thought, find out if any division is present, anywhere.

Is it real or is it imagined?

On present evidence, is there a 'you' that sees the moon – or is there simply the seeing of the moon? Now drop the concept of 'the moon' and what's left? What's left when the one who sees collapses into what is seen?

This is about looking deeply into your own experience – and then telling the truth. If you don't know, admit you don't know – until you can know – because I must tell you, you *do* know.

This holds true of anything you look at. There's just one movement, without any separation. Despite your firm belief it has been three movements, it was never split into a seer that sees the moon; you just assumed the division.

The truth is, there is only seeing, without any subject-object division.

You are the activity of Seeing and Knowing Itself – inseparable from what is seen. Separation is simply a thought based in your limited perceptual capacity. The five senses weren't designed to see This, but we continue to believe what our senses tell us.

No-boundary awareness is direct, immediate and non-conceptual. It is absolutely uncompromising and not mere philosophical theory. This is why the Sages and Mystics all agree that Reality is beyond name and form, beyond words and descriptions – and beyond division and boundary.

Since Oneness created the mind to divide and separate, it makes perfect sense that the mind asserts, "It is I that sees the sight." The only thing you are absolutely certain of is that you are. The knowing that you are expresses through the mind as the thought "I am," but you can't ever pinpoint where this separate "I" is.

No doubt has ever arisen here since 2004, when it was finally seen that separation was the Daddy of all the illusions. When it was finally seen that "I" am not living my life – and that "I" never did, all that contracted energy identified with a personal self dissolved back into boundless energy of what I Really am.

If I had a belief about what I am, doubt would *have to* arise. It's not possible to engage in belief without having some degree of doubt. It's simply the way it works.

When it was finally and truly seen that I never had a life, and that the One Life is living this life, all doubt dropped away. What dropped away in that seeing was the contracted energy that believed in the mental image called 'me.'

In its place, a boundless energy moved in, without an identity and yet, inseparable from anything. You could say liberation is "an energetic shift" from the personal contracted energy to the impersonal boundless energy – a shift in identity from the 'little me with a little world' to the 'Big One,' without a world.

In that energetic shift, a radical shift in perception moved in and has never left. I didn't do any of it. Seeing what was true 'did' the work. Once it was seen that there wasn't any center, the shift happened spontaneously. Where once the unknown made "me" uncomfortable, the unknown is now Home.

All psychological and emotional insecurity was completely gone, and in its place, a deep yes with everything, as it is. It is very difficult to express in words and as a result, is usually misinterpreted. In truth, it can only be misinterpreted. After all, 'it' can only be truly understood within, experientially, not conceptually.

A deep no can arise with what is, but it's not a problem because a deep yes lies beneath it.

In attempting to share this with others, it is usually received as a new belief system or way of thinking that "I created" in order to live more comfortably in "my" own skin. Because this is totally beyond belief and conceptualization, this reception is understandable.

As much as you don't want your loved ones to suffer anymore, you can't make them want to see what they really are. You can't make others want peace and freedom more than anything else.

Life is living through them, too – perfectly and appropriately. There is no ladder to climb or wall to scale.

Everyone really is perfect just the way they are.

When it is finally seen, beyond belief, what you are, it's not that you are suddenly in possession of extraordinary powers and psychic abilities. You don't necessarily become the most compassionate person in the world, either – nor do you walk around in constant bliss showering everyone you meet with love beyond measure.

Life goes on as before, only now it is without the inner division and struggle. Resistance can still come up, but it is seen through rather quickly. You don't wish it were any different. As a result, suffering doesn't arise.

Those close to you typically don't notice that something has happened.

They may have a sense that something is different, but they cant quite put a finger on it. This can only be understood from the inside, not from the outside looking in.

In the absence of any ego that drives a life, others noticing isn't important. There isn't any need here for anyone to notice this remarkable and incomprehensible transformation. Ultimately, none of it really matters. Anyway, I digress.

No longer was there any real concern about anything anymore. No longer was there any energy going into the dream of being an individual separate from anything else, because it was finally seen that there is no one home, and that there was never anything personal going on.

Separation was seen to be unreal – and simply imagined.

Thus, what was there to fear? Who was present to fear anything? What remained was simply Life, and it was living through me, as me – and much better than 'I' ever could.

You can confirm in your own experience that there is nothing personal going on. Granted, it sure appears that way, but this isn't about appearances. Isn't this about going beyond appearance and concepts, to the Reality behind? See that everything is illusion with a certain life span, except for what you are.

You are The Reality.

Illusion doesn't mean it isn't there. Illusion means that it appears and disappears with a particular life span and therefore, can't be real.

The Real never comes and goes.

While you appear to be a separate person with a separate soul, you are in fact, the One Soul appearing as a separate person.

There's only one thing going on. There is only One Being in many forms, none of which is separate from each other. This is the enlightenment you are looking to discover.

There is One Singular Consciousness peering through the eyes of ALL life, including the most tyrannical dictator to the most compassionate person.

Consciousness is all-inclusive. It peered through Hitler's eyes just as much as Mother Theresa's eyes. It is looking through every animal, mammal, bird, bat, shark and alligator – and Is That at the same time.

There is only one animating essence energy behind every life form – and YOU are that. Not a "part" of that, but That in it's entirety, wholly and completely.

Don't believe a word you read here.

See what is real, and not what is imagined.

And then the permanent shift in perception will happen all by itself – and there's nothing personal about it.

Chapter 23
My Song Is Silence

"Only when you drink from the river of silence will you really sing."
– Kahlil Gibran

There is a song playing in the background – listen closely. Can you hear it? In fact, it is stuck on repeat, endlessly playing. Because it never began, it never ends. Because it is ever-present, it is easily overlooked. It is a song of silence, and its melody is so sweet and gentle.

Silence is the source out of which everything springs from, abides in, and returns to. It is the formless, underlying essence that continually gives birth to thought forms, like the ocean continually gives birth to waves. As no wave ever harms the ocean, no thought can ever impact what you really are.

Always arising and falling, waves arise from the Source Ocean, always being an expression of the Ocean. Upon returning to the Ocean, they forever remain one with the Ocean.

Though it appears the wave "returns" to the ocean, it never left the ocean. Wave and ocean are inseparably one. Silence, thought and activity are one. Silence is not the opposition to thought, noise and activity, but the ever-present, unchanging background of all thought, noise and activity.

Even a bird singing 'tweet, tweet' and your dog barking is a perfect expression of absolute silence, a song of the vast spaciousness. Oh, how silence sings!

Silence is beyond the opposites, allowing absolutely everything to come and go in its stillness, never clinging to or resisting any of it. Silence welcomes all, without bias or rejection, and is the most gracious Host, never making any demands, never insisting on silence.

Nothing ever obstructs this silence. Nothing *can* obstruct the silence you are. You see that no thought can disrupt the Silent, Awake Being that is your Original Nature. Why would the ocean mind if it has big waves or little waves, whether its surface is calm or turbulent?

Regardless of the appearance at the surface, the depths are unaffected by whatever goes on at the surface.

Silence is the Ground of Being.

There is no need to *make* yourself quiet. Before you look to facilitate quiet, notice that it is already quiet. Any movement towards creating silence is manufactured. Any movement to acquire silence only reinforces the illusory idea that silence isn't already fully present – and that you aren't already that silence.

Silence is prior to, in the midst of, and after each thought, feeling and activity. It never leaves. It is here right now as you read this. Ever-changing weather simply passes through the background of the empty, silent sky.

Changing thoughts, feelings and activity appears in the unchanging, background of the ever-present silence you are.

Silence isn't separate from Awareness; they are one.

Silence threatens to reveal what's unreal.

Everything that drops away in silence is unreal.

It's amazing what drops away when you are silent.

Running from an overactive or condemning mind, silence is often something avoided at all cost. Movies, television, books, video games, cell phones and the Internet all become a source of refuge for those seeking to avoid the mind's litany of ideas, judgments and aversions.

Ironically, the refuge they really seek is what they are running from.

Notice that the mind reverts back to silence spontaneously after each experience. Notice every experience happens within an ever-present background of silence. Without silence, nothing is.

Listen to the silence you are, and trace all thinking, feeling and activity back to its source.

Can you 'find' anything? You won't find anything, but what do you discover? What always remains?

What remains is the Silent Empty Awareness, full of the passing scene. It is without division or boundary – and everything comes out of it and falls back into it.

Silence is the mind's natural state, abiding as the substratum that all thinking occurs in. Can you even imagine existence without silence? Can you imagine your mind *not* being able to fall into silence? Would you want to?

Whether we realize it or not, we count on silence. In the absence of silence, we'd go mad. In the absence of silence, we'd never know what we are. Appreciate silence, for without it, you'd never have the opportunity to see what you are.

You'd never have the ability to enjoy all the beauty and magnificence You offer on full display if it were not for silence.

Every story you have about yourself arises out of the story-less silence you are. All stories told are old. Silence is always fresh and brand new.

Be still and know the silence you are. Listen to silence; it's what you are.

There is only timeless Being,
the inexplicable mystery of what you are.

What You're Looking For Is What Is Looking

You are both the Source and Essence of all,
always, already – without any condition.
Resting as unchanging awareness, peace and joy,
You manifest as all changing worlds and beings.
There is no requirement to be what you are.
Instead, simply be what you are.
Drop the struggle and end the fiction
and see the wisdom in
the lazy man's way.

There is no effort needed to see what is actually here.
What effort is needed to arrive at the effortless?
Let go of the assumption you are a limited body/mind
Possessed with a particular lifespan.
In the silence of awareness that you are,
turn 180-degrees around and face your Self,
surrender the "I" thought
and see you've always been free.
Recognize it's all been a dream,
that happened to no one.
I am the silence in the song
and the song in the silence.
And it sings so beautifully.
My song is silence.

Chapter 24
A Single Eye

"Looking in a mirror, I appear to be looking out of two eyes, while 'here' there is only one eye."

– Douglass Harding

Let's take a closer look at a few beliefs the vast majority of us would agree on as true, and *see* if they are actually true. Let's investigate something that we automatically believe is true, pretty much from childhood on.

Imagine that you are the only human on the planet – yes, just you, all alone.

In fact, it was always just you and you alone. Imagine that there aren't any animals or other creatures with seeing eyes that are looking back at you. There are no lakes, rivers or oceans, either. There isn't anything in your field of vision that could serve as a mirror to see yourself, including shiny objects.

Consequently, you have no idea what you look like because there isn't anything to see your reflection, to see what you look like. I realize that this isn't a vision of the most attractive planet to be living on, but this is just hypothetical, so bear with me.

So, you're just sitting there, relaxing your gaze, looking out at the landscape of trees, the sky and the ground.

Are you there in your imagination right now? With these particular conditions around you, how many eyes would you say you're looking out of?

Now remember, you can't see yourself and you have never seen another human being or animal in your life. How many eyes would you say you were looking out of? Is it two or one? In actuality, you don't even have to imagine this lonesome scenario.

You can do this without referring to thought or the past.

Find out in your own direct experience, right now.

Discover what present evidence actually reveals.

If you relax your gaze and take in the entire visual field, without moving your eyes, allow yourself to become aware of the edges of the visual field. You'll notice an oval-shaped window that you're looking out of.

You are indeed looking through a single eye, not the two you've assumed for so long.

Granted, our whole lives we look out and see people with two holes in their head looking back at us. We see our reflection in mirrors, lakes and rivers – and we've been taught to believe we've been looking *out* of two eyes simply because we possess two eyes.

In reality, we've been looking out of a single eye. Two eyes appear as separate, but there is only One Vision, one seeing, and one knowing.

It is The One appearing as two.

So, your whole life you've *believed* that you've been looking through two eyes, but in reality, you haven't. If you really *see*, you'll see that all along you've been looking through one eye and not the two you believed in.

Granted, you possess two separate eyeballs and can see through both, but in essence and not appearance, you are looking through one eye.

Could this be the "third eye" several traditions point to? What other beliefs do you operate from that aren't true – that never *were* true? If this is indeed true in your direct experience, what other long-held beliefs do you cling to?

If you say the ocean is blue, could you bring me a container full of blue water? The point is this: our senses trick us into believing the appearance of things. Finding out what you are is a game of looking beyond appearances to the underlying essence.

This is beyond any appearance; this is beyond the senses.

Chapter 25
Who Dies

"The real does not die, the unreal never lived. Once you know that death happens to the body and not you, you just watch your body falling off like a discarded garment. The real you is timeless and beyond birth and death. The body will survive as long as it is needed. It is not important that it should live long."

– Nisargadatta Maharaj

Life and death are two sides of the same coin. Without death, there is no life. What could be more natural than the physical death of something that is born to die? What could be more natural than the death of that which was never meant for eternal life? How can that which is made of perishable stuff survive?

Are we really locked inside the prison of our body/mind, or are we the unbounded awareness that the body is within? Are we really a separate personality with a separate mind trying to make our lives work? See that what you are is not inside of the perishable body – but that the perishable body is inside you.

When we can see our body and notice thinking occurring, being the witness of them, are we not already inextricably free from all movement and sensation? Are we not *already* free from what we witness?

How is it that we've identified our Original Identity with that which is seen and therefore, must perish?

When we rest in the witnessing awareness, watching all thoughts and sensations passing through, can we not sense the innate freedom and release, a sense of not being bound by the continuous parade of concepts and images witnessed?

Resting in the clear and open space of awareness, can we see that the Original Witnessing is not "out there" in the stream of time and objects? Can we see that what we are is the vast and empty background in which all the streams of time and objects arise?

What are all objects appearing to? What are they appearing in? Don't come up with a conceptual answer.

Simply pause, look and sense.

Consciousness was not created with the body – and will not perish after the body dies. In fact, it never enters the stream of time and therefore, isn't subject to death. It does not live on *after* the body dies, for it lives *prior* to the body.

Because it is Unborn, it is Undying.

What has always intrigued this author is the fear engendered at the thought of death. Somehow, it was always sensed here that death wasn't real – and that it was just something we all assumed was real, like taxes.

To this day, it's probably why I love cemeteries so much. When I look at them, it's a reminder not of "my" and "your" eventual demise, but that there isn't anyone who dies. It's a peaceful yard where bones are buried. It's a reminder that what is born indeed dies – but You and I were never born.

When I am in a graveyard, I see the end of suffering for so many who believed they had a life. I see an appearance of death, but no actual death. I know that no personality ever died, because it never existed other than a thought. When I am in a graveyard, I am in total peace, because there isn't a shred of doubt in what I am.

While there might be a spontaneous physiologic contraction of fear in this body/mind at the sudden sight of driving off a steep cliff, that contraction will undoubtedly happen in the realization that death is just a concept.

I am the Unborn, Formless Eternal One – the One without a second, in which the cycle of birth and death continually repeats itself. I remain untouched and prior to such cycles. I am the fountain in which all cycles spring from and repeat.

Does this mean that great sorrow won't arise when a loved one dies? No, it doesn't. Grief will certainly arise and great sorrow will surely be experienced for as long as it must – but suffering can't happen because it won't be resisted.

It will be experienced deeply without the filter of the mind that says 'this shouldn't have happened,' 'why so soon,' or 'I just can't live without them.'

Suffering is the result of the grasping and avoiding of the separate self, and what ends it is the realization and transcendence of the separate self. Suffering is an inevitable byproduct in the knot or contraction known as the personal self, and the only way to rid suffering is to see through the personal self.

Seen through, painful experiences no longer own you anymore; they aren't a problem.

If you don't discover this before your physical death, there is nothing to worry about. The discovery is imminent upon the death of the body. It doesn't really matter one way or the other, but if you desire to know who dies, or if you have a good amount of psychological fear surrounding your eventual physical demise, then it might be useful to see who dies now.

To clarify, there isn't a "who" that dies. Rather, 'what' dies is more the question.

Once there is a clear recognition that what you're looking for is beyond you, there is a readiness to die. Goethe said, *"As long as you do not know how to die and come to life again, you are but a sorry traveler on this dark earth."*

That's a bit harsh, but you get the point.

So who dies? Rather, what dies?

The death of the body/mind is essentially the ending of the dream of separation and individuality; it is the ending of the story of a "me" that was trying to always make its life work, journeying a path in time, focused on becoming the 'best person' it could become.

Christian mystic Meister Eckhart said, *"The kingdom of God is for none but the thoroughly dead."*

What dies is the firm conviction that you are a separate entity living in a world apart from you, that you are a body/mind organism with name and form. What follows physical death is the resurrection and realization of what you've always been.

Upon physical death, all ideas of heaven, hell, the afterlife, reincarnation, karma, reward and sin end in the clear recognition that there was never anyone living a life and therefore, these concepts never applied. All ideas of here and there, now and then and before and after die in the realization there's only a timeless now, without any location.

All beliefs and autobiographical stories die, too. Every one of them, no matter how much they were cherished.

Naturally, the personality has a very difficult time accepting the fact of its own disappearance, and invents a story about an afterlife or reincarnation.

Many believe in an individual soul created at birth that transcends physical death, and that it is 'going somewhere' after the body's last breath. Perhaps it's heaven if you were a "believer," or maybe it's purgatory or hell if you weren't.

Why do we want to know what we'll be (and where we'll be) when we die, instead of wanting to know what we are now? The solution to our future problem lies in the present.

Why don't we expend our energy and attention on finding out who is it that dies? Why don't we find out what dies – before physical death – instead of making up stories about who we think we are and where we're going? To me, this is the classic case of "putting the cart before the horse."

Why can't we admit that these unquestioned, unproven stories are simply strategies to comfort and assuage ourselves?

Refusing to imagine its own demise, the mind will go to any measure to believe in a story that speaks of continuation after the death of the body. Since there is no "before" life, there is no "after" life. Life is always now, outside the stream of time, welcoming all stories without ever trying to get rid of any of them.

If it is all one, with nothing in opposition, what concern is there?

Life doesn't need your prayers. In this moment, Life accepts you unconditionally, just as you are, exactly as you are not. It has no concept of salvation, redemption, forgiveness, sin, imperfection or worthiness.

The only appropriate prayer is, "Lord, help me to accept your will, not mine – and open my eyes, Lord, and help me to see as You see."

This timeless discovery is the death of the search for anything outside of yourself, for you finally see you *are* all of it, and never once apart, or other than any of it.

Chapter 26
A Love So Radiant

"Seeing that one is nothing is wisdom; seeing that one is everything is love, between the two my life moves."

– Nisargadatta Maharaj

All there is, is
This appearing as that,
Subject appearing as object,
Absolute appearing as relative
Impersonal appearing as personal

Truth appearing as illusion
Stillness appearing as all movement
Security manifesting as need and want
Compassion appearing as judgment
Cradled in an unconditional love beyond all comprehension.

What You're Looking For Is What Is Looking

All there is, is
Wholeness appearing as division
The Unknown appearing as the known
Boundlessness appearing as limitation
Uncaused Joy appearing as suffering

Freedom appearing as Bondage
The Hopeless appearing as hope
Total Poverty appearing as acquisition
Absolute Humility appearing as grandiosity
Embraced in an unconditional love beyond conceptualization.

All there is, is
The One appearing as two,
The Unseen appearing as the seen,
The Nothing appearing as everything,
The Uncaused appearing as the caused

Emptiness appearing as fullness,
Unicity appearing as separation
The Unborn appearing as the born
The Unconditioned appearing as conditioned
Forever held in the arms of the Beloved.

All there is, is
What is happening
In a Love So Radiant,
Self-Shining of its own accord
Never adequately put into words.
It can't ever be sought after
If you look for it you won't find it.

It can be avoided, rejected or forgotten
Conceptualized, believed in and worshipped.
It can never be taught, learned or given,
Taken away, hidden away or lost.
It can't be attained or compromised,
Nor can it be harmed or approached.

It is silence making noise and stillness causing movement.
It is the wordless appearing as words, reflecting back to the wordless
To remember all there is, is This That You Are
All in a Love So Radiant.

Chapter 27
No Goal But This

"If you could get rid of yourself just once, the secret of secrets would open to you. The face of the Unknown, hidden beyond the universe, would appear on the mirror of your perception."

– Rumi

Being inseparable from anything, there isn't anywhere to go and nothing to grasp or avoid. Being intimately available for all sensation and experience, there is nothing to work out, fix or improve.

Not a single particle of dust is excluded from this Magnificence; no object, whether sacred or profane, painful or frightening, is excluded from this embrace, for each and every thing is equally and eternally the Radiance of Divine Spirit.

Never wanting or needing anything other than what shows up, you bask in the Witnessing of the wonder, beauty and perfection of Life, as it is. Never moving towards or away from any of it, you behold the Majesty and Grace of every single thing in the universe.

Every event, every happening and experience is welcomed in the passionate arms of The Beloved, That Which You Are.

Being Choice-less Awareness, all is seen in the Light of true understanding, never to be run from or chased after, for you are all of it, unfolding the way it's meant to unfold. No longer needing anything, it is discovered you are everything.

Being the empty container for all content to come and go in, you are forever free from harm, reveling joyously in the mere fact of existence.

The unending Play of Consciousness, without beginning or end, moves through you unimpeded by any obstruction whatsoever – caressing your Original Face like a baby's touch. All prior defense mechanisms and strategies dissolve in the defenseless Refuge you are.

Having uncovered every lie, misconception and belief, all that's left is bare-naked awareness, inextricably free from anything at all. In this freedom without location or condition, the seeming veil of separation is lifted leaving just This and nothing else.

Where once so much energy and attention was placed towards trying to fit in, now it's impossible not to recognize The One everywhere and in everything.

No longer needing to cultivate the qualities of Spirit – peace, love, compassion and love spontaneously arise without any desire for them to show up. You are already the qualities that you were seeking, and in the absence of seeking, a joy without cause and an undefended heart is your Guiding Light.

No longer feeling that you are an entity located inside a body here and now, it is seen that there is only a timeless presence, not a 'now' – and 'here' as location-less presence, and not any location in space. No experiencer and no experience. There's only This – and it is beyond time. The emptiness of Consciousness recognizes itself as the fullness of This.

Wholly unconcerned, yet intimately engaged, there is absolutely nothing to fear or recoil from, for you are each and every thing, entirely and completely. Everything you look at is what you are, and in this boundless seeing, you are released from everything you were once bound by.

And in this unshakable knowing, all struggle and effort dissolves in your loving gaze. Resting in This, there is no goal but This. A poem by Rumi:

Didn't I Tell You...
Didn't I tell you
Do not leave me for I am your only Friend,
I am the spring of life.
Even if you leave in anger for thousands of years
You will come back to me for I am your goal and end.
Didn't I tell you
Not to be seduced by this colorful world,
For I am the Ultimate Painter.
Didn't I tell you
You are a fish do not go to dry land,
For I am the deep Sea.
Didn't I tell you
Not to fall in the net like birds,
For I am your wings and the power of light.
Didn't I tell you
Not to let them change your mind and turn you to ice
For I am your fire and warmth.
Didn't I tell you
They will corrupt you and make you forget
That I am the Spring of all virtues.
Didn't I tell you
Not to question my actions,
For everything falls into order, I am the Creator.
Didn't I tell you
Your heart can guide you home
Because it knows that I am your Master.

Chapter 28
No Place Like Home

*"That which is before you is it, in all its fullness, utterly complete.
There is naught beside. Even if you go through all the stages of a
Bodhisattvas' progress toward Buddha-hood, one by one; when at last,
in a single flash, you attain to full realization, you will only be realizing the Buddha-Nature which has been with you all the time; and
by all the foregoing stages you will have added to it nothing at all."*

– Huang Po

Being Home is the clear recognition that home is wherever you are.
You are the Home you've been seeking – and you never left. In fact,
you can never leave what you are. Being home already, no path or process needs to be undertaken in order to *be* home.

You are the love and beauty you've been seeking. Being Home is
the realization that the substance of your Home is *built* from Love and
Beauty. Love is the discovery that others are not others. Beauty is the
discovery that objects are not objects.

Love and beauty is what you are.

Being Home is the realization that there is only what is happening –
and that there isn't anyone it's happening to. While the mind continues

to separate and divide what is inseparable, Life simply happens.

When it is seen that you are before the mind – and when it is seen that the mind is an object in Consciousness that is known, the mind has a tendency to quiet down. In silence, the mind finally sees its limitations and bows to its source, knowing its true place and function.

Resting in the simple, clear and alive presence of awareness that everything is dependent upon, there is an extraordinary absence of the person you used to think you were. In that absence is a presence intimate with all that arises.

You are the open, unchanging capacity for all things to intimately arise in.

What you are has no need to alter this moment. It has no need to be certain of anything, for you are the certainty in the uncertainty – and you are the uncertainty in the certainty. What you are bathes in the wonder of the unknown.

All uncertainty is fully embraced in the certainty you are.

If this moment is unknown, with an infinite potential of outcomes, how can the moment be predetermined?

Although whatever arises cannot be any other way than it is, this inevitable moment doesn't imply destiny. If there is any destiny, it is in the "things are always as they are" Reality. This is precisely what Anthony de Mello meant when he described enlightenment as an *"absolute cooperation with the inevitable."*

All thoughts, feelings and sensations appearing presently are already welcome in the vast, open, spacious awareness that you are. Nothing is denied or avoided; nothing needs to be modified or improved. Nothing needs to be purified, forgiven or worked through. This moment is whole and complete, as it is.

In fact, You *are* this moment, unfolding exactly as it is.

There is no place like Home. Even if you feel you aren't Home, you never left Home. There has never been any real obstacle in the way of you being Home. It is only a thought that divides the seamless totality of experience into an experiencer and the experienced.

Being Home has no concept of getting rid of doubt, unease, anxiety or fear. All emotion and dis-ease are allowed to arise in the doubt-less, fear-less, feeling-less space of Home you are. Resting in the unconditional love you are, you are the Love for the unloved. Resting in absolute and total security, you are the Home for the homeless.

You are the untouched, timeless Home for all time-bound experience to rest in, no matter how painful or frightening. Whatever arises is being fully embraced – by what you are. You don't need to "do" surrender. Simply and effortlessly notice surrender is what you already are.

What you are offers no resistance to anything, ever.

The mind's resistance or rejection to anything that arises is an after-thought, a delayed response to what already is, to what is already being allowed. The mind's reactions and interpretations are totally irrelevant to what you really are – and can never impact the empty Space of awareness you are.

When it is seen that you aren't who you believed yourself to be, you're no longer a person with a background or history. You're not a man, woman, father, mother, brother, sister, son or daughter. You're not a husband, wife, Christian, Jew, Buddhist, Hindu, Muslim, agnostic or atheist.

You're not Black, White, Asian, Indian, Latino or any other race. You're not a happy or depressed person. You aren't a rich or poor person, a successful or unsuccessful person. You are not your body or mind that will one day perish.

You are the Home for all identifications and misperceptions to rest in.

Your Real Identity isn't any object that appears in Consciousness. You don't even possess a face, kidneys, a heart, a spine and lungs. You don't own eyes that see, ears that hear, a nose that smells, hands that touch and taste buds that taste. Before these things, you are.

You are prior to all known perceptions.

You are the knowing activity of all perception itself.

You are the Unconditioned, Content-free Awareness that all conditioning and content arises in.

You are not any concept or idea you could ever come up with. You are the wordless actuality they all point to. Before thought, you are. Before words, you are.

You are Life itself; never were you an individual entity possessing a life. You never lived in this world; the world was always within you. You are the awareness that is inseparable from everything that arises in awareness.

Not only are you the awareness of all that arises, you are what arises, too. Everything that appears is made of the Same Singular Substance.

Like all waves are made of the ocean, whatever arises is made from the awareness it arises in.

Like the wave that reaches the shoreline ceasing to be a wave, it is revealed to be the Ocean all along. Seeking and thoughts of resistance and desire cease in the clear light of understanding, and is revealed to be sourced in that which produced it – the clear, open space of presence you are.

That Space is the Home that cannot be named or described.

Resisting and avoidance strategies die out in the nameless Subject, the Subject that allows what is. Only in temporary name and form did they seem to have an independent existence apart from the Home that I am. Clearly seen, they arise not in another's home, but in my Home.

They are always welcome Here.

And yet, dropping all concepts, there is just This and nothing else. There is just what's happening. There is always just what is happening – prior to the mind's commentary about what is happening, without description, name and form. Nothing needs to be rejected, denied or ignored.

Why would it?

It's all One, whole and complete within itself.

Even if identification happens with an illusory individual, you are no less the One Life, appearing as a seemingly separate individual. While it appears personal, there is nothing personal unfolding. It's impersonal – and it's universal.

You aren't doing any of it, including reading or trying to understand this right now.

Being free means being empty of the idea of separation.

Being free means being empty of the idea of owning a body and a mind.

Being free means being empty of the idea of possessing anything at all.

There is more than enough room for the entire Cosmos Here. Nothing is left out and all is welcome, equally and without condition.

Everything you see is what you are.

From the old man shuffling down the street pushing a cart of groceries, the wrinkles in your father's skin, your heart breaking at the thought of your dear mother trying to come to terms with a progressive, incurable disease, a homeless man in tattered clothes rummaging through a dumpster for food, to a mother breast feeding her baby – all that you see is what you are.

If you deny this, it simply means you just believed a thought in your mind. It simply means that you believe the thoughts in your head *as* Reality, and that you believe separation *is* the Reality.

How can you deny what you don't understand and yet see? What sense does it make to reference the temporal, death-bound and dependent mind for Truth or Reality?

This is what everyone is seeking, whether they know it or not, but can't seem to find.

It is so ordinary and immediate – and so readily available.

It is so radically simple that it can't be taught, learned, formulated or given.

It is not of this world, but it is nothing but this world.

It is the snow falling on Christmas eve, the wind howling on a crisp, autumn day, dogs barking, car horns sounding, lovers arguing, the pain in the chest as the body dies, women shopping and women chatting on the phone.

It's men watching Sunday football, men fishing, children playing, animals on the prowl, enemies killing, villagers pillaging, natives poaching, the sun setting and the night falling.

It is anger arising at the sight of an elderly woman being pushed out of the way by a middle-aged man trying to pass her down the steps, and finding yourself rushing over to make sure she doesn't fall, because you had no choice, and you never did have any choice.

Seeing that you were never once separate from anything, that you never once chose your thoughts and behaviors, you finally see that choice and free will are illusory. Finally seeing that you are being lived by the One Life, and that you never had a life, the contracted energy of the fictitious self disperses back into the boundless energy you've always been.

In that dispersing, a radical shift in perception occurs and you're no longer identified with the 'I' thought and the body. You *see* what Jesus meant when he made the statement, "I and my Father are One" – and Saint Francis of Assisi's pointer, "What you're looking for is what is looking." It makes you tilt your head to the sky and laugh out loud.

What I was looking for was here all along, closer than breathing, nearer than hands and feet – and it was doing the looking. "Who" would of thought? What a great place to hide something so obvious. No wonder it was overlooked for so long.

"He is hidden in His manifestation, manifest in His concealing."

All the pent up guilt, shame, blame, resentment and remorse accumulated from an imagined past simply dissolves in the clear recognition that none of it is real, and none of it was ever real, including the "you" that imagined all that – including a "you" with a past, present or future.

You are the timeless now that everything arises in. Not only are you this moment, you are all that arises *in* this moment.

In place of insecurity and low self-esteem, absolute security and a complete absence of *any* self-esteem whatsoever moves in. Where before you had a lingering sense of incompleteness and inadequacy, now there is an abiding sense of fullness – and a deep OK-ness with what is, as it is.

There is a transparency felt now. Arrows of insults and other harsh words can be slung in your direction, but since there is no receiver of them, there is no landing spot for them. In come the arrows in the front – and out through the back they go.

Nothing sticks. Nothing ever did stick; it just felt that way. This is what it means to be beyond harm.

It's not opposed to anything, because it *is* everything, even opposition to opposition.

And this transparency isn't just reserved for negativity. It is for absolutely everything, including thoughts, feelings, sensations and experience. Having no solidity at all, it is recognized that everything is energy.

Having no solidity at all, you are free to experience the full gamut of Life, both the ups and downs, without ever identifying or taking ownership of any of it.

And all is allowed to move through the empty space you are, making room for the next experience.

Home is total poverty; Home is total humility and absolute acceptance.

And still, there is an intimacy felt with all of it. Experience tends to be richer and fuller because all is welcome in My Home. Nothing is avoided and nothing is chased after. Being the empty capacity for all that passes in front of Me, nothing lasts, and nothing can harm me.

Reality is what is – and you are that, wholly and completely, now and eternally.

All arguments cease in the seeing that what is seen is what you are. The eye that sees God is the same eye God sees with.

No teachers, no students. No awake or unawake beings. No path or absence of a path. Simply life loving itself, spontaneously dancing all by itself, appearing as the seen and unseen, rising and falling back into the empty, aware, knowing Space that allows it all to be, eternally.

Free at last, free at last.

There's no need to click your heels. There never was.

There's no place like Home.

Only a separate mind would desire more.

Only a separate mind would desire something other.

You're already Home.

You know you're Home when the question whether or not you're Home drops away.

Since you're Home, there's nowhere to go.

Everything is a celebration of the Infinite Eternal.

And although words weren't ever necessary to realize this,

No more words are needed now.

Simply rest in what you are.

You *are* Home.

CPSIA information can be obtained at www.ICGtesting.com
Printed in the USA
LVOW11s1730010415

432909LV00005B/611/P